The
Remarkable
Stories
Behind the
Naming of
Texas Towns

The National Mule Memorial in downtown Muleshoe.
Courtesy of Ray Miller.

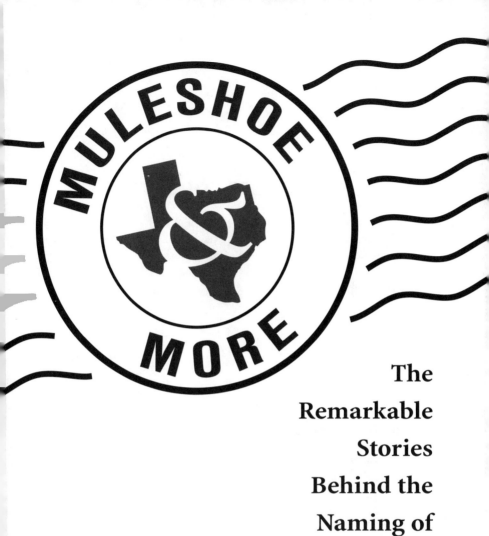

MULESHOE & MORE

The
Remarkable
Stories
Behind the
Naming of
Texas Towns

Bill Bradfield and Clare Bradfield

Gulf Publishing Company
Houston, Texas

Muleshoe & More

Copyright © 1999 by William H. Bradfield.

Printed in the United States of America.

Gulf Publishing Company
Book Division
P.O. Box 2608 □ Houston, Texas 77252-2608

10   9   8   7   6   5   4   3   2   1

Library of Congress Cataloging-in-Publication Data
Bradfield, Bill, 1927–
    Muleshoe and more : the remarkable stories behind the naming of Texas towns / Bill Bradfield and Clare Bradfield.
        p.   cm.
    Includes bibliographical references and index.
    ISBN 0-88415-865-9 (acid-free paper)
    1. Names, Geographical—Texas—Anecdotes.   2. Cities and towns—Texas—Anecdotes.   3. Texas—History, Local—Anecdotes.
I. Bradfield, Clare.   II. Title.
F384.B73   1998
917.64′003—dc21   98-27975
                                                              CIP

Preface

Welcome to the world of Texas town names. The study of place names has a specialized name of its own—toponymy (tah-PAHN-uh-mee)—and there's no better place to sample it than Texas, a fertile field because of the state's immense size and variety. You will find *Muleshoe & More* to be a quick and lively reference guide with an A-to-Z listing of towns. Be warned, however, that more careful exploration of these pages could turn you into a Texas toponymic expert in your own right.

The Texas map, like the state's broad landscape, offers great contrasts, exemplified by the intermingling of languages and cultures that goes back to earliest Texas history. Most of the towns were founded more than 100 years ago, and many of their names originated much like those of towns elsewhere:

Borrowed names—communities named for towns or cities in other states or countries. **Family names**—places named to honor individuals or families, among them war heroes, public officials, early settlers, postmasters, storekeepers, or railroad engineers. **Descriptive names**—names describing the areas in which the towns are located or chosen simply because they sound pleasant. **Geographic names**—names taken from rivers, lakes, mountains, and other landmarks. **Botanical names**—names of trees and other plant life prominent when the towns were settled.

But these broad categories omit the many Texas towns with names derived from cultural sources including the Bible and religion, popular and classic literature, and mythology. Nor do they reflect the intermixture of languages that results, for instance, in three towns named Sweetwater: the Nolan County seat with the English name; the Nueces County town (Agua Dulce) with a Spanish name, and the Wheeler County town (Mobeetie) whose name comes from a Native American language.

Bigfoot and Whon, although named for persons, have monikers that do not quite fit the pattern of family names. That's surely true of Topsey, a name taken not from one of the residents but from his favorite mule.

And how do you classify Ding Dong in Bell County? Bug Tussle? Gun Barrel City? Pep? Dime Box? Cut and Shoot? Bebe? Domino? Each has its own unique story.

Preferred pronunciations are shown for town names that are often pronounced incorrectly, such as Mexia and Refugio. These pronunciations, appearing as phonetic respellings, were published previously in our *Texas Towns From A to Z Pronunciation Guide*. The stressed syllables are indicated by capital letters. Population figures shown for the towns are current estimates obtained from the Texas State Data Center and other sources in 1998. The postmarks that illustrate the text come from Texas post offices, which have played no small role in the naming of Texas towns.

Invariably, the persons we approached while working on this book went out of their way to give every possible kind of information we sought, and offered it with courtesy and kindness. Among these were postmasters, librarians, newspaper editors and reporters, genealogists, Chamber of Commerce managers and staffers, city and county officials, and officers of town and county historical societies. We are grateful to one and all.

Our gratitude goes also, for many and varied reasons, to Laurel Laurentz, Larry Howell, F. E. "Ab" Abernethy, Robert M. Thomas, Clay Bradfield, and Elizabeth Hedstrom.

ABILENE
West central Texas • Taylor County • 117,061

C. W. Merchant named Abilene, founded in 1881, after Abilene, Kansas. He and other ranchers marketed cattle in the Kansas town and hoped its Texas namesake would become equally important. The ranchers and land speculators picked a townsite on the new Texas & Pacific Railway line, and at auction more than 300 lots were sold in two days. In 1883 citizens voted to incorporate the town, and Taylor County residents selected Abilene as the county seat.

ACE
Southeast Texas • Polk County • 40

This settlement dates back to the 1830s and was known for decades as Smithville. Its post office closed in 1871 and reopened in 1915—but this time Washington postal officials wouldn't accept Smithville as its name, since a Smithville post office already existed in Bastrop County. Instead, they gave both post office and town the name Ace, for Postmaster Asa "Ace" Emanuel.

ADDISON
North central Texas • Dallas County • 11,800

Addison, a burgeoning suburb of Dallas in the 1980s and 1990s, began in 1904 as a post office at a St. Louis Southwestern Railroad depot. Its name derives from the postmaster, Addison Robinson. Addison remained one of Dallas County's smallest towns for a half century, but from the 1970s on the suburb experienced full-scale metropolitan development. Since the early 1980s Addison Airport has ranked as the third busiest general aviation airport in the nation.

AFTON
Northwest Texas • Dickens County • 15

This community was called Beckton early in the 1890s and Cottonwood late in the 1890s. A Cottonwood post office already existed in Callahan County, so, according to one West Texas historian, the name Afton was suggested by Mrs. R. L. Sitton, who had moved here from Afton, Oklahoma. Another source contends that a beautiful stream flowing through town led schoolteacher Myra Kelly to propose the name of the river in the old song "Flow Gently, Sweet Afton."

1

Agua Dulce

Gulf Coast • Nueces County • 871 • ah-wuh DOOL-sih

Agua Dulce's Spanish name, meaning "sweet water," derived from a Nueces County creek. A settlement developed here around the 1890s, and oil and gas were discovered in this vicinity in the late 1920s.

Alamo

Far south Texas • Hidalgo County • 11,853

Some local historians say Alamo was named to honor the San Antonio mission that became a Texas shrine; some sources point to the area's giant cottonwood trees (*alamo* in Spanish); others note that the Alamo Land & Sugar Company bought the townsite in 1909. The town's population began to grow in the mid-1930s and early 1940s as Alamo developed into a shipping center for citrus fruit and vegetables and a winter resort and retirement town.

Alanreed

Panhandle • Gray County • 48

In the late 1880s and early 1890s, Panhandle settlers knew this community by several names: Prairie Dog Town, Spring Tank, and Gouge Eye, the latter for a memorable saloon fight. During this period, a townsite was established, with a post office called Eldridge. A surveyor for the Choctaw, Oklahoma & Texas Railroad laid out a nearby townsite in 1900. Its name combined (changing the spelling somewhat) the names of the Allen & Reed rail contracting firm's partners. The lure of the railroad soon attracted residents of Eldridge, and their post office, to relocate here.

Alba

Northeast Texas • Rains and Wood counties • 538

The Missouri-Kansas-Texas Railroad built its line through this vicinity in 1881. As a result, the area's settlers became a community, with telegraph service and a post office. Local lore holds that the town's name—the Spanish word for "white"—was chosen because settlers would not permit blacks to move into the vicinity. Another source says Alba was named for a railroad official's son.

Albany
West central Texas • Shackelford County • 1,985

About 20 states have towns called Albany. William R. Cruger, who assisted in organizing the Shackelford County government, named this town for his birthplace, Albany, Georgia. Chosen to replace Fort Griffin as the county seat, Albany welcomed the Texas Central Railroad's arrival in 1881—an event that ended the town's role as a supply point for trail drivers en route to Dodge City but made Albany a rail shipping point for cattle.

Alice
South Texas • Jim Wells County • 20,625

Settlers arrived in this area around 1850 and formed a small community about three miles from the present town. In 1883, with the construction of a railway depot and a new townsite to develop, residents applied for a post office, to be named for rancher R. J. Kleberg. Postal officials pointed out that a Kleberg post office already existed, so the applicants proposed the name Alice, in honor of Kleberg's wife.

Alief
Southeast Texas • Harris County • 1,400 • AY-leef

In 1895 W. D. Twitchell platted this townsite, and a successful application was filed for a post office, named for Postmaster Alief Magee. By 1900, the town's population passed 100, but the great Galveston hurricane and massive flooding wiped out most of the community and its farm crops. Metropolitan growth later turned Alief into a residential suburb, which was partially annexed by Houston in the 1970s.

Allen
North central Texas • Collin County • 35,650

First settled in 1870, this town grew as the Houston & Texas Central Railway extended northward from Dallas in 1872. The town was named for Ebenezer Allen, a native of Maine who migrated to Texas in the 1830s, served as attorney general and secretary of state of the Republic of Texas during Anson Jones' 1844-45 presidency, and in the 1850s was a promoter and manager of the H&TC railroad. Allen was a rural community until the late 1960s when population and commercial activity spread out from the Metroplex.

An old view of Mitre Peak, Alpine. Courtesy of Houston Metropolitan Research Center, Houston Public Library.

ALPINE

Southwest Texas • Brewster County • 6,088

This community in the Rio Grande River's Big Bend was first called Osborne and later Murphyville. After it was designated as the county seat, settlers petitioned Washington to change the post office name to Alpine, because of the town's location in the Davis Mountains at an elevation of 4,484 feet. The change became official in 1888.

ALTAIR

Southeast Texas • Colorado County • 30

Altair was named by an amateur astronomer, Curly Jones, for a star in the constellation Aquila. Local legend has it that someone quipped the name would be appropriate because the area's cowboys often were "all on a tear."

Alto

East Texas • Cherokee County • 1,053

In Spanish and Latin, *alto* means "high." Henry Berryman is credited with proposing the name this town adopted in 1852 because of its location on a high divide between the Angelina and Neches rivers.

Alton

Far south Texas • Hidalgo County • 3,536

Alton originated in 1911 as a stop on the San Benito & Rio Grande Valley Railway. Railroad men named the citrus growing and farming community for the Alton Railroad, founded by residents of Alton, Illinois.

Alvarado

Central Texas • Johnson County • 3,355 • al-vuh-RAY-doh

William Balch, who established a trading post on a trail across eastern Johnson County, laid out a townsite here in 1853. The town's first law officer, A. H. Onstott, proposed the name Alvarado, recalling the site of his combat experience in the Mexican War.

Alvin

Gulf Coast • Brazoria County • 20,457

Alvin was named for Alvin Morgan, a native of Louisiana who settled here in 1879, built a general store and saloon on his property, and established a post office in a railroad boxcar. Although cattle raising was always important to Alvin, around the turn of the century the town also became a major producer of strawberries. W. S. "Ole" Benson and his brother, C. W., who shipped strawberries from Alvin, are credited with the idea of using blocks of ice to refrigerate a freight car so they could ship fresh strawberries a greater distance. Gulf, Colorado & Santa Fe Railway officials liked the innovative proposal and the first refrigerated shipment was made in 1895.

Amarillo
Panhandle • Potter and Randall counties • 174,143 • am-uh-RILL-oh

It required a second townsite to get Amarillo started, but the effort produced the largest city in the Texas Panhandle. Amarillo was named for Amarillo Creek, so called by Mexican herdsmen because of its yellow banks and the abundant yellow wildflowers there. In 1887, when the Fort Worth & Denver City Railway was building tracks across the Panhandle, T. J. Berry moved here and platted a townsite on the railroad right-of-way. A mile to the east, rancher Henry Sanborn and his partner, Joe Glidden, platted another townsite, claiming Berry's site was vulnerable to flooding. Heavy rains in 1889 proved them right and the fledgling community relocated to the site on higher ground. Amarillo was a major cattle-shipping point by 1892, when the town incorporated. Cattle continue to be important to Amarillo's economy, along with agriculture, oil, and natural gas. For several years, Amarillo was also the world's sole producer of helium.

Amherst
Northwest Texas • Lamb County • 745

Amherst originated as a station for William Halsell's Mashed O Ranch in 1913, when Halsell granted right-of-way to the Pecos & Northern Texas railroad. A railroad official named the town for Amherst College in Massachusetts. Population totaled 749 in 1940 and has dipped only slightly since.

Anahuac
Gulf Coast • Chambers County • 2,252 • AN-uh-wac

The first settlement here on the northeast bank of the Trinity Bay was Fort Anahuac, a Mexican fort established around 1821 to control the entry of American colonists into southern Texas. Development of the town began decades later, and Anahuac became the county seat in 1908. Various legends trace the origin of the town's name to an Aztec word meaning "plain near the water"; to the name of an Indian chief, Anahwa; or to Nahua, the Aztec language still spoken in parts of Mexico.

ANDERSON
Southeast Texas • Grimes County • 370

In 1846 Henry Fanthorp donated land for the townsite of this county seat. After weekly mail delivery to his Fanthorp Inn began, he became the community's first postmaster. Fanthorp named the town and post office in honor of Kenneth L. Anderson, last vice president of the Republic of Texas, who died at the Fanthorp Inn while campaigning to be elected governor of Texas. With a strategic location on the stagecoach route, Anderson attained a population of 3,000, making it briefly the fourth largest town in Texas. By the mid-1990s its population was one-tenth that number.

ANDREWS
New Mexico border • Andrews County • 10,531

Like the county, this town was named for Richard Andrews, a hero of the Texas Revolution who died fighting in the Battle of Concepcion on October 28,1835. The town was chosen as county seat in 1910 and incorporated in 1937.

ANGLETON
Gulf Coast • Brazoria County • 20,241

Lewis Bryan and F. Kiber founded Angleton in 1890, acquiring land for a townsite and selling lots to prospective residents. The partners also traded an interest in the townsite to the Velasco Terminal Railway in exchange for construction of a rail line through Angleton and a depot in the town. Angleton was named for Mrs. George Angle, wife of the general manager of the railway.

ANNONA
Northeast Texas • Red River County • 357 • an-NOH-nuh

This town was first called Walker Station, for its founder, George W. Walker, but changed its name to Annona in 1884. According to some accounts, Walker suggested the town be named "for a beautiful Indian girl," but the name may have been generated by a Washington postal official instead. Perhaps it was inspired, with a subsequent misspelling, by the Indian heroine of Helen Hunt Jackson's popular 1884 novel *Ramona*. Another possibility is that Dr. George G. Wooten suggested the name Annona, asserting that it meant "depot" or "supply point" in Latin.

ANSON

West central Texas • Jones County • 2,689

This town, first called Jones City, became the seat of Jones County in 1881. Both were named for Dr. Anson Jones, a participant in the Battle of San Jacinto and last president of the Republic of Texas. Because other Texas towns were also named for Jones, County Surveyor Martin Duvall recommended the town instead honor Jones by taking the name Anson.

ANTHONY

Far west Texas • El Paso County • 3,727

As an unincorporated community straddling the Texas-New Mexico state line, this place was first known as La Tuna, for the federal prison located here. The post office moved across town from New Mexico to Texas in 1942, and the Texas side incorporated in 1952. The town's name is ascribed to a nineteenth-century shrine dedicated to St. Anthony of Padua.

ARANSAS PASS

Gulf Coast • San Patricio, Aransas, and Nueces counties • 8,072

This fishing and shrimping town was first named Aransas Harbor but changed its name to Aransas Pass in 1892, taking the name of the entrance to Aransas Bay. Historians say a Spanish explorer, Joaquin de Orobio y Basterra, named the pass in honor of "Our Lady of Aranzazu" in 1746.

ARCHER CITY

North central Texas • Archer County • 1,976

Like its county, this county seat was named for Dr. Branch T. Archer from Virginia, who fought for Texas independence in the battle at Gonzales and later served as Speaker of the House of Representatives for the fledgling Republic of Texas. Archer City and its movie theater, the Royal, were the setting for Larry McMurtry's 1966 novel, The *Last Picture Show,* and for the critically acclaimed 1971 movie version. The author, who grew up in Archer City, opened a bookstore there called the Blue Pig, later renamed Booked Up. By 1997, McMurtry's store had more than 100,000 volumes and occupied four buildings.

The Royal movie theater, Archer City, after it closed in the 1960s. Courtesy of Ray Miller.

ARGYLE
North central Texas • Denton County • 2,161

According to one story, pioneer settlers named this place for their former home town in Clinch County, Georgia. Another version is that Bill Brown, a well-traveled Texas & Pacific Railway man, picked the name, recalling the beautiful Argyll area of Scotland.

ARLINGTON
North central Texas • Tarrant County • 301,700

Arlington, a suburb that grew in the 1990s to be more than half the size of Fort Worth, dates back to the 1870s when the Texas & Pacific Railway was preparing to extend its tracks from Dallas to Fort Worth.

In 1875 the new post office was named, although not permanently, for Andrew Hayter, a Presbyterian minister who surveyed this area at the railroad's request. It was renamed Arlington, after the Virginia home of General Robert E. Lee, in 1877.

ARMSTRONG
Gulf Coast • Kenedy County • 20

This rural community was named for rancher John B. Armstrong. During a short but action-packed career in the Texas Rangers, Armstrong took part in the breakup of outlaw gangs along the Rio Grande border and captured the notorious gunman John Wesley Hardin with three of his gang members. He was also involved in the slaying of train bandit Sam Bass at Round Rock. The small settlement here originated after the St. Louis, Brownsville & Mexico Railway built a station in 1904 to serve the Armstrong Ranch. Throughout its history, Armstrong has consisted primarily of the railway station, a post office, and some nearby dwellings.

ARP
Northeast Texas • Smith County • 966

The International & Great Northern Railroad built its tracks through this area in 1872, leading settlers to form a community they called Jarvis Switch. A post office opened here with the name Strawberry, chosen because local growers had begun shipping strawberries via the railroad. In 1899, Postmaster C.P. Orr announced the post office had a new name that, with just three letters, would allow strawberry shippers to label their boxes more quickly. Was someone from Georgia involved in the name selection? Arp was named in honor of Bill Arp, a popular columnist for the daily *Atlanta Constitution*.

ART
Central Texas • Mason County • 18

Known first as Willow Creek, this little community became Plehweville in 1886, after Otto Plehwe, first postmaster. In 1920, postal officials asked Postmaster Eli Dechart to submit a name that was shorter and easier to spell. Dechart proposed the last three letters of his own name: Art.

ATHENS

East Texas • Henderson County • 11,692

Athens was established in 1850 on a site selected by a board of land commissioners for the new county seat. It was given the name Athens at the suggestion of Dulcena "Aunt Dull" Avriett, who remembered Athens, Alabama, her home town, as a center of culture and learning. Some East Texas historians claim Athens was named instead for Athens, Georgia; others contend it was named for Athens, Greece, from which the Georgia and Alabama towns both derived their names.

ATLANTA

Northeast Texas • Cass County • 6,160

Ten miles from the Arkansas state line, this town was settled after the Texas & Pacific Railway extended its tracks here in 1872. It was named for Atlanta, Georgia, former home of many of the early settlers.

AUBREY

North central Texas • Denton County • 1,360

Originally called Onega, the community was renamed when its post office was established in 1881. Residents who didn't like the original name wrote down three suggestions on slips of paper, placed them in a hat, and Aubrey was the name drawn. Why it was suggested is not known.

AUSTIN

Central Texas • Travis County • 572,288

Austin was named for Stephen F. Austin, the "Father of Texas," a native of Virginia who served the Texas republic as secretary of state under President Sam Houston. The original townsite lies in what was called Stephen F. Austin's "little colony." From 1839 to 1842, this town was capital of the Texas republic, and in 1850, after Texas joined the United States, its voters selected Austin as their permanent capital. At the time, Austin's population was 854.

11

AVALON

Central Texas • Ellis County • 130 • AV-uh-l'n

Avalon, the mythical island paradise where King Arthur recovered from his battle wounds, reputedly was suggested as the name for this landlocked town by an early settler.

AVOCA

West central Texas • Jones County • 121 • uh-VOH-kuh

Spring Creek was the first name of this community, but its post office, established in 1893, was named Avo. Merchant J. L. Crostwaite, whose general store housed the Avo post office, appended two letters to the post office's name. He apparently drew his choice from Irish poet Thomas Moore's lyric poem "Avoca," which contains the line "Sweet vale of Avoca."

AZLE

North central Texas • Parker and Tarrant counties • 10,699

A post office named O'Bar opened here in 1881. Two years later, the post office and its growing community adopted the name Azle in honor of Dr. Azle Stewart, a physician and landowner, who contributed land for the townsite. Population exceeded 1,000 in the 1940s and later grew to more than 10,000, as Azle benefited from light manufacturing, its proximity to Eagle Mountain Lake, and suburban housing developments.

BACLIFF

Gulf Coast • Galveston County • 6,211 • BAY-klif

This town developed from a summer beach resort into a well-established residential community, known as Clifton-by-the-Sea. But when an application was filed in 1950 to establish a post office here, postal officials in Washington pointed out the name was too long to fit on a rubber cancellation stamp. So they selected Bacliff, a name with only seven letters.

Balch Springs
North central Texas • Dallas County • 18,700

Around 1870, John Balch and his family settled here on land where they discovered three flowing springs. For almost a century, the name of the community they founded was pronounced like the family's name: "bawlk." But the town's population has nearly quadrupled since 1970, and the newer residents tend to pronounce the name "bawlch" instead.

Ballinger
Central Texas • Runnels County • 4,292 • BAL-in-jer

This town was established when the Gulf, Colorado & Santa Fe rail line extended into Runnels County in 1886, and was named after one of the railroad's prominent stockholders: William Pitt Ballinger, a Galveston lawyer and former federal district attorney who was twice appointed to the Texas Supreme Court and twice declined.

Balmorhea
West Texas • Reeves County • 816 • bal-moh-RAY

When this town in the Toyah Creek valley was founded, someone figured out that it could be named to honor the three land promoters: E. D. Balcom, H. R. Morrow, and J. E. Rhea. Balmorhea, the name of the post office that opened here in 1908, combined the first syllables of Balcom's and Morrow's names with the last three letters of Rhea's name.

Bandera
Southwest Texas • Bandera County • 1,271 • ban-DEHR-uh

A settlement called Bandera formed here in 1853. When the county organized in 1856, it adopted the same name, a Spanish word meaning "flag" or "banner." The town may have been named for the famous Bandera Pass, site of a fierce battle between Texas Rangers and Comanches, or for a Spanish general who led a campaign against Apache Indians who had raided San Antonio.

BANGS

Central Texas • Brown County • 1,609

Founded in the 1880s, Bangs was named for Samuel Bangs, a pioneer printer and newspaper publisher who once owned the land that became the site of this town's general store. In 1817 Bangs produced some of the first documents printed in Texas, and he later published newspapers in Galveston, Corpus Christi, and Houston.

BANQUETE

Gulf Coast • Nueces County • 449 • ban-KEE-tih

Banquete is a Spanish word meaning "banquet" or "feast," and this town was named for just such an event—but local historians differ on when and why it was held. According to one version, the town got its name in 1832 when early settlers from Ireland arrived and were welcomed by Mexicans living in this area, who prepared a feast on a creek bank. Another version refers to a four-day feast held to celebrate the completion of a road connecting San Patricio, Texas, with Matamoros, Mexico.

BARRETT

Southeast Texas • Harris County • 3,452

Barrett was named for its founder, Harrison Barrett, a former slave who settled his family here after emancipation, bought land in 1889, and established a black community originally known as Barrett's Settlement. The Barrett family set up a sawmill and gristmill, established farms in the vicinity, and donated a site for Shiloh Baptist Church.

BASTROP

Central Texas • Bastrop County • 5,673 • BASS-trahp

Bastrop was named in 1837 for Felipe Enrique Neri Baron de Bastrop, land commissioner of Stephen F. Austin's colony and member of the Congress of Coahuila y Texas. A soldier of fortune, Bastrop became an influential citizen of San Antonio and used his influence with the Mexican government to enable Moses Austin to obtain the land grant for an Anglo-American colony in Texas. Although he claimed to be a native of Holland and son of a Baron de Bastrop, historians have concluded his real name was Philip Boegel and that he was a fugitive born in Dutch Guiana.

BAY CITY
Gulf Coast • Matagorda County • 18,829

The Bay City Townsite Company established this town in 1894, when the county seat was moved here. The decade that followed brought railroad service, electricity, and the beginning of rice production. Bay City incorporated in 1902 with about 2,000 inhabitants.

BAYTOWN
Southeast Texas • Harris County • 71,282

Nineteenth-century settlers had a small sawmill and general store near Galveston Bay and called their settlement Bay Town. Neighboring Pelly

Oil derricks in Baytown, 1920. Courtesy of Houston Metropolitan Research Center, Houston Public Library.

annexed the town and then consolidated with nearby Goose Creek in 1947. Voters decided to name their combined city Baytown; it became a major center of the petrochemical industry.

BEAUMONT
Southeast Texas • Jefferson County • 115,242 • BOH-mahnt

In 1835 Henry Millard and two partners bought fifty acres to develop as a townsite here. Three years later, the first Congress of the Republic of Texas designated the new town of Beaumont as the seat of newly organized Jefferson County. The town may have been given Mrs. Millard's maiden name, Beaumont, or the name of a merchant, Jefferson Beaumont of Natchez, Mississippi, possibly related to one of the Texas settlers. The Spindletop discovery well started an oil boom here in 1901.

BEBE
South central Texas • Gonzales County • 52 • bee-bee

W. G. Bair, a grocer who became Bebe's first postmaster, is credited with naming this little village in 1900. According to local lore, he was trying to think up a town name when he noticed the name of a brand of baking powder on a nearby shelf.

BEDFORD
North central Texas • Tarrant County • 48,300

Weldon Bobo, who established a general store and a gristmill here after the Civil War, proposed that this community be named Bedford after a county in his native Tennessee. Bedford lost population and even its post office during the first half of the twentieth century, but a surge of urban growth began in the mid-1950s.

BEEVILLE
South Texas • Bee County • 14,327

Beeville took its name for Bernard Elliott Bee, Sr., who came to Texas from South Carolina in 1836 and joined the Texas revolutionary army. He was one of three commissioners chosen to take Santa Anna, the defeated Mexican president and commander, to Washington, D.C. Later, Bee served as the Texas republic's secretary of war, secretary of state, and minister to the United States.

BELLAIRE
Southeast Texas • Harris County • 15,018

When in 1909 W. W. Baldwin, vice president of the Burlington Railroad, began promoting the sale of property in the new town he established here, he named the town for Bellaire, Ohio, one of the towns on the Burlington rail line. Bellaire remains an independent city, although Houston now surrounds it on all sides.

BELLEVUE
Oklahoma border • Clay County • 351

Bellevue began as a shipping point on the Fort Worth & Denver City rail line in 1882. One of the railroad officials gave the town its name because it reminded him of the view from his window at Bellevue Hospital in New York City, where he had once been treated.

BELLMEAD
Central Texas • McLennan County • 8,500

This community on Waco's northeast side was originally a railroad town, created in the mid-1920s when the Missouri-Kansas-Texas line established its locomotive shops here. It was named after Belle Meade, the famed Kentucky horse farm.

BELLS
Oklahoma border • Grayson County • 1,034

Originally called Gospel Ridge for its many churches, this town was renamed Bells because its church bells rang so loudly in celebration when the Texas & Pacific Railway began operation here in 1873.

BELLVILLE
Southeast Texas • Austin County • 3,840

Thomas B. Bell and his brother James emigrated from Florida in 1822 to become part of the "Old Three Hundred"—the 300 families who received land grants in Stephen F. Austin's first Texas colony. They began farming in the area of the future Bellville townsite, which was developed about a quarter century later. Bellville's population grew rapidly after the arrival of the Gulf, Colorado & Santa Fe rail line. The many Germans among the newcomers built an opera house and founded a weekly German-language newspaper in 1891.

BELTON
Central Texas • Bell County • 14,020

Bell County, named after Governor Peter Bell, was established in 1850. Fourteen months later, the Texas Legislature changed the name of the county seat from Nolanville to Belton, condensing the words "Bell" and "town."

BEN ARNOLD
East central Texas • Milam County • 148

This town, originally a stopping point on the San Antonio & Aransas Pass Railway established in 1890, was named for three-year-old Bennie Arnold. Her father was notarizing documents for the township company's purchase of land along the railroad right-of-way when he was asked to pick a name for the town.

BENAVIDES
South Texas • Duval County • 1,858 • ben-uh-VEE-dez

Benavides was named for Placido Benavides, a rancher who donated an 80-acre tract to this community in 1881 after earlier giving permission for a Texas Mexican Railway depot to be constructed on his land. The rancher was a veteran of the Civil War and the nephew of another Placido Benavides, who earned a place in Texas history a half century earlier by aiding the Texas revolutionary army. In Victoria County, the town of Placedo and Placedo Creek were named, with a change in spelling, for the elder Benavides.

BEN BOLT
South Texas • Jim Wells County • 110

In 1904 L. R. Collins, a major landowner, laid out this town near Alice, the county seat. When residents applied for a post office, Collins suggested the name of a popular ballad, "Ben Bolt." The song included the line "Don't you remember sweet Alice, Ben Bolt?"

BENBROOK
North central Texas • Tarrant County • 21,500

After the Texas & Pacific Railway built tracks to the southwest part of Tarrant County in 1876, the settlement of Miranda changed its name to Benbrook. The name honored James Benbrook, a county resident who was influential in persuading the railroad to route its trains through here. In the second half of the twentieth century, Metroplex suburban development boosted the once-rural town's population dramatically.

BEN FRANKLIN
Northeast Texas • Delta County • 75

More than a century ago, after the Gulf, Colorado & Santa Fe Railway built its route through Delta County in 1886, Ben Franklin was a busy town with a thousand residents. The town developed on the land grant of Benjamin Simmons, one of the first settlers, and was named for his son.

BEN HUR
East central Texas • Limestone County • 100

Early settlers called this village Cottonwood, but it gained a literary name when its post office opened in 1895. A. R. Derden proposed the name Ben Hur after reading the popular semi-biblical adventure novel.

BEN WHEELER
Northeast Texas • Van Zandt County • 400

Mail was carried many miles from Tyler on horseback to reach early settlers in this area. When this community developed sufficiently for residents to seek their own post office in 1878, they proposed that it be named for Benjamin F. Wheeler, the horseback rider who brought the mail to them.

BIGFOOT
South Texas • Frio County • 75

When a post office was established here in 1883, it was named for legendary Texas Ranger William Alexander Anderson "Bigfoot" Wallace, a

Texas Ranger "Bigfoot" Wallace. Courtesy of Houston Metropolitan Research Center, Houston Public Library.

resident of the town. During its early years, Bigfoot consisted of a general store, a small public school, a church, and scattered houses. In the 1950s, a small oil field in the vicinity boosted the number of residents to more than 200, but population fell again after the early 1970s.

BIG LAKE
West Texas • Reagan County • 3,344

Big Lake's name comes from a large, dry lakebed that became a lake during infrequent spells of rainy weather in this part of West Texas. The town developed in 1911 along the Kansas City, Mexico & Orient Railroad's new tracks through Reagan County. After driller Carl Cromwell struck a gusher with the Santa Rita well near here in 1923, the county seat was transferred to Big Lake and population rose quickly. The Santa Rita was the first big find in the Permian Basin, one of the world's great oil regions.

BIG SPRING
West Texas • Howard County • 23,699

A big, refreshing spring in the Sulphur Draw was an oasis for Indian hunting parties, herds of buffalo and other animals, and West Texas pioneers. A trailblazer from New Mexico, Captain Randolph Marcy, chose it as a campsite in 1849 and described it as "the big spring of the Colorado." When the Texas & Pacific Railway built its westward line along a stretch of Sulphur Draw in 1880, settlers near the spring moved to the rail line and the town of Big Spring was born.

BIROME
Central Texas • Hill County • 31 • bye-ROHM

Birome was founded in 1910 on ranchland owned by R. L. Cartwright of Waco. Its name came from the given names of Cartwright's sons, Bickham ("Bi") and Jerome ("rome").

BISHOP
Gulf Coast • Nueces County • 3,429

Bishop's founder, Corpus Christi insurance agent F. Z. Bishop, bought a large tract of Driscoll Ranch land and developed it as a master-planned model town in 1910. The amenities he provided—streets and sidewalks, a sewer system, waterworks, an electric power plant, telephone lines, a three-room school, a hotel, and retail space—quickly attracted residents.

BLANCO
Central Texas • Blanco County • 1,576

The Pittsburgh Land Company donated 120 acres of land as a townsite for the seat of newly organized Blanco County in 1858. The town was also named Blanco, "white" in Spanish, after the Blanco River which has a bed of white limestone in many places. Though the rival town of Johnson City won an 1890 election to replace it as county seat, Blanco remained a farm and ranch trade center.

BLANKET
Central Texas • Brown County • 443

Blanket was named for nearby Blanket Creek. According to local legend, in 1852 a surveying team found several blankets left on the creek bank by Tonkawa Indians who had been hunting buffalo.

BLEIBLERVILLE
Southeast Texas • Austin County • 71 • BLYE-bler-vil

Bleiblerville, a small village settled by German and Czech families in the 1880s, took its name from Robert Bleibler, whose general store became the center of the community. A post office opened in Bleibler's store in 1891 and he became Bleiblerville's first postmaster.

BLESSING
Gulf Coast • Matagorda County • 571

Grateful that the Galveston, Harrisburg & San Antonio Railway was being extended into this area in 1903, landowner Jonathan E. Pierce submitted an application for a post office, to be named "Thank God." Postal officials approved the application, but turned down the name; later, they settled on "Blessing" as a compromise.

BLOOMING GROVE
East central Texas • Navarro County • 867

According to local lore, this community's name came from a nearby grove of oak trees surrounded by bluebonnets. Another version has it that a grove of trees belonging to Blooming Davis, an early settler, was known as "Blooming's Grove."

BLOSSOM
Northeast Texas • Lamar County • 1,638

An abundance of beautiful wildflowers led this area to be called "Blossom on the Prairie," later shortened to Blossom Prairie, when a post office opened in 1849. The name was shortened again—to Blossom— in 1888, two years after the town incorporated.

BOERNE
South central Texas • Kendall County • 5,901 • BER-nee

When John James and Gus Thiessen laid out the townsite for this community in 1852, the latter named the town for writer and satirist Ludwig Boerne. Boerne's outspoken criticism of the German political order was popular with Thiessen and other German immigrants but so unpopular with the authoritarian German government that the writer chose self-exile in France. A post office opened here in 1856, and in 1862 the little town was designated the seat of Kendall County.

BOGATA
Northeast Texas • Red River County • 1,398 • buh-GOH-duh

James E. Horner intended to name this town's post office after Bogota, capital of Colombia, but a clerk in Washington had trouble reading Horner's handwriting on the application form. When Horner received official notice of his appointment as postmaster in 1881, he discovered the name had been approved as Bogata. Residents still pronounce the name as if Horner's intended spelling had been retained.

BONHAM

Oklahoma border • Fannin County • 7,023 • BAH-num

A community on Bois d'Arc Creek became the seat of Fannin County in 1843 and was named in honor of James Butler Bonham, who died defending the Alamo. It later developed into a farming center served by both the Texas & Pacific and the Missouri-Kansas-Texas railroads.

BON WIER

Louisiana border • Newton County • 475 • bahn WEER

The Kirby Lumber Company established Bon Wier in 1905 and named it for lumbermen B. F. Bonner and Robert W. Wier. Later, the town of Wiergate was also named after Wier.

BORGER

Panhandle • Hutchinson County • 15,708 • BOHR-ger (hard "g")

Capitalizing on the discovery of oil in this vicinity, in 1926 A. P. "Ace" Borger and a partner developed a 240-acre townsite, which Borger named for himself, and promoted it as an oil boomtown. Their sensational advertising attracted more than 40,000 people within three months. Borger was a lawless Wild West town for several years until Governor Dan Moody, using emergency powers, dispatched state officers to rid Borger of its criminal element.

BOVINA

Panhandle • Parmer County • 1,783 • boh-VEE-nuh

Originally this place was the Hay Hook line camp of the giant XIT Ranch. Cattle for eastern markets were loaded onto rail cars here, and train crews referred to the settlement as Bull Town. But when a post office was established in 1899, the name was given a Latin or Spanish twist: Bovina. For a time, Bovina shipped more cattle than any other point in the world.

BOWIE

Oklahoma border • Montague County • 5,404 • BOO-ee

When the Fort Worth & Denver City Railway built its tracks through here in 1882, settlers moved to this location and laid out a townsite. They named the town for James Bowie, who was killed at the Alamo.

BRADY

Central Texas • McCulloch County • 6,144

Brady took its name from Brady Creek, which runs through the town. The creek was named for Peter Rainsford Brady, who was born in Washington, D. C., in 1825 and lived an adventurous life as a soldier, surveyor, public official, and Texas Ranger. The town of Brady became the county seat in 1876 and grew as an agribusiness market.

BRAZORIA

Gulf Coast • Brazoria County • 3,134

John Austin, a good friend and possibly a distant relative of Stephen F. Austin, established Brazoria in 1828. He said he selected the town name because he knew of none other like it anywhere in the world.

BRECKENRIDGE

North central Texas • Stephens County • 5,917

When Stephens County organized in 1876, the town of Picketville was chosen as the county seat and was renamed in honor of John Cabell Breckinridge, who served as vice president under James Buchanan from 1857 to 1861. In the process of renaming the town, the spelling of his name was altered to Breckenridge.

BRENHAM

Southeast Texas • Washington County • 13,585

Brenham became the seat of Washington County in 1844, just a year after it changed its name from Hickory Grove to honor Dr. Richard Fox Brenham, who served in the Texas revolutionary army and died fighting as a member of the Mier expedition in 1843. Blue Bell Creameries, the town's best-known enterprise, began in 1907 when townspeople used an abandoned cotton gin to churn farmers' excess cream into butter. Although only distributed regionally, Blue Bell was the nation's third-best-selling brand of ice cream in 1997.

BRIDGE CITY

Louisiana border • Orange County • 8,446

This town originated as a settlement called Prairie View. It was renamed Bridge City after the $2.6 million Rainbow Bridge, spanning the Neches River, was completed in 1938. The bridge expanded highway connections to nearby petroleum and shipping center Port Arthur.

BRIDGEPORT
North central Texas • Wise County • 4,013

Bridgeport acquired its post office and name in 1873, when an iron bridge was constructed to span the West Fork of the Trinity River. Twenty years later, the Chicago, Rock Island & Texas rail line reached this area and the town moved a mile to benefit from the railroad location.

BRONTE
West central Texas • Coke County • 956 • brahnt

Bronte, founded in 1887, is one of several Texas towns named for writers—in this instance, Charlotte Brontë, best known as the author of *Jane Eyre*. Pronunciation of the English novelist's name took a distinctly Texan twist, however.

BROOKSHIRE
Southeast Texas • Waller County • 3,512 • BROOK-sher

Brookshire formed in the early 1880s along the Missouri-Kansas-Texas Railroad. The town was named for Nathan Brookshire, who received title to a league of land as a member of Stephen F. Austin's fifth colony. A native of Tennessee, he served in the War of 1812 before coming to Texas and later fought against the Creek Indians in central Texas.

BROWNFIELD
Northwest Texas • Terry County • 9,213

Land promoters bought and developed a section of land here in 1903, naming the town for the prominent Brownfield ranching family and offering a free business lot to anyone who would build a store or a shop. In 1904, by a margin of five votes, Brownfield was chosen over Gomez as the county seat. The town developed as an agribusiness center through the 1920s and 1930s, later boosted by oil field activity.

BROWNSVILLE

Far south Texas • Cameron County • 134,267

This town's history goes back to the latter part of the eighteenth century, but its name comes from the fort established here by General Zachary Taylor's soldiers in 1846. Taylor sought to confirm the Rio Grande as the U.S.-Mexico national boundary. First called Fort Texas, the stronghold later took the name Fort Brown in honor of Major Jacob Brown, who died during an attack by Mexican troops. Through the years, Brownsville emerged as an important international market center, benefiting first from railway connections and later from its airport, international bridge, port, and ship channel.

Fort Brown, Brownsville. Courtesy of Ray Miller.

Brownwood
Central Texas • Brown County • 19,534

Brown County and Brownwood are named for Captain Henry S. Brown, who commanded a military company at the Battle of Velasco, an 1832 fight between Texas and Mexican troops. Brownwood was chosen as county seat in 1857. Its population increased markedly in the 1920s, with oil exploration and production, and during World War II, when Brownwood's Camp Bowie grew into the largest military training center in Texas.

Bruni
South Texas • Webb County • 581 • BROO-nih

Bruni became a station on the Texas Mexican Railway around 1881. It was named for Antonio M. Bruni, an Italian immigrant, who began ranching in this area in 1877 and later served as county treasurer for 35 years.

Bryan
Southeast Texas • Brazos County • 62,330

William Joel Bryan, a nephew of Stephen F. Austin, donated land for this townsite in 1865 and granted the Houston & Texas Central Railroad a right-of-way to build tracks into the town. Texas A&M College opened nearby at College Station in 1876, and by 1900 Bryan's population exceeded 3,500.

Buda
South central Texas • Hays County • 2,081 • BYOO-duh

Buda is a corruption of the Spanish word *viuda,* meaning "widow." The name was supposedly inspired by a widow operating a small hotel here in 1887, when this town's post office opened.

Buffalo
East central Texas • Leon County • 1,975

Founded in 1872, when the International & Great Northern Railroad established a station here, this town was named for the great buffalo herds that earlier roamed Texas and other midwestern and western states.

BUFFALO GAP
West central Texas • Taylor County • 530

Buffalo Gap owes its name to the bison that found Elm Creek as a watering hole and to the buffalo hunters who camped here during the winters of the 1860s and 1870s. A trading post was established in the vicinity about 1870, and Buffalo Gap, the community that grew up around it, became the seat of newly formed Taylor County in 1878.

BUG TUSSLE
Oklahoma border • Fannin County • 15

This small community's post office, which was open only from 1893 to 1894, was named Truss for early settler John Truss. Some time after the post office closed the community became known as Bug Tussle. Local lore says the name arose after a summer when the area's picnic grounds proved equally attractive to picnickers and swarms of bugs.

BUNA
Southeast Texas • Jasper County • 2,443 • BYOO-nuh

The Beaumont Lumber Company founded this community as a base for its Jasper County mill operations around 1890 and obtained approval for a post office in 1893. Joe E. Carroll, Sr., logging manager for the lumber enterprise, submitted Buna as the post office name to honor his cousin Buna Corley.

BURKBURNETT

Oklahoma border • Wichita County • 11,218 • berk-ber-NET

Theodore Roosevelt reportedly arranged to have this town's post office named for rancher Samuel Burk Burnett in 1907. Burnett had been host to the president and other guests during a wolf hunt at his big Four Sixes ranch.

BURLESON

Central Texas • Johnson County • 19,412

The Missouri-Kansas-Texas Railroad platted a townsite for Burleson in 1881 on the railroad's proposed route from Fort Worth to Hillsboro. The Rev. H. C. Renfro, a Baptist minister, sold the townsite to the railroad and was allowed to name the depot. He called it Burleson in honor of his mentor, Rufus C. Burleson, who later served as Baylor University president from 1886 to 1897.

BURNET

Central Texas • Burnet County • 4,511 • BERN-et

In 1852, when this county was created and named for lawyer-politician David G. Burnet, the town of Hamilton became the county seat. The legislature changed the town's name to Burnet in 1858, pointing out that there was another Texas town named Hamilton. Burnet shipped carloads of red granite for construction of the state capitol at Austin between 1882 and 1888.

CACTUS

Panhandle • Moore County • 1,949

Cactus began in May 1942 as a World War II industrial town, housing Chemical Construction Company employees while they built a military defense plant. The 10,000-acre site first had to be cleared of a vast amount of thorny cactus, inspiring the name company engineers gave to this location, and the name of the plant itself: the Cactus Ordnance Works.

CALDWELL

East central Texas • Burleson County • 3,775

The name of this county seat honors Mathew Caldwell, an early Texas revolutionary leader and signer of the Texas Declaration of Independence, who was known as "Old Paint" because of his spotted whiskers.

Surveyor George Erath laid out a townsite here in the 1840s, and the Republic of Texas established the town's post office. The Gulf, Colorado & Santa Fe Railway reached Caldwell in 1880, transforming the town into a shipping point for all Burleson County.

CAMERON
East central Texas • Milam County • 6,006

At its founding in 1846, this town was named for Ewen Cameron, a native of Scotland who served two terms in the Texas army. He became a leader of the 1843 Mier Expedition party, which was captured by Mexican troops. Its members were each forced to draw a bean from a jar. Those who drew black beans were executed. Cameron drew a white bean, but was shot anyway in an attempt to escape.

CAMP WOOD
Southwest Texas • Real County • 833

The United States Army's frontier outpost Camp Wood, established in 1857, provided protection against Indian raids for travelers between El Paso and San Antonio and for settlers in the Rio Grande Valley. It later served as a Confederate camp during the Civil War. In 1920, the town of Camp Wood took shape when the Uvalde & Northern Railroad made this location its northern terminus.

CANADIAN
Panhandle • Hemphill County • 2,451

The Canadian River, which flows by this town, is said to be named for the Canadian traders who bought furs along the river's route through Colorado. Developed in 1887 as the seat of newly organized Hemphill County, Canadian attracted residents through promotional advertising and the construction of a river bridge to nearby Hogtown, whose inhabitants soon relocated here.

CANTON
Northeast Texas • Van Zandt County • 3,449

Canton, the seat of Van Zandt County, was founded in 1850 by settlers moving here from a Smith County community called Old Canton. The name Canton comes from its definition, "a small territorial division of a country."

CANUTILLO

Far west Texas • El Paso County • 5,109 • kan-yoo-TEE-yoh

This town originated around 1909 and was named for the Canutillo Ranch, established in this area in the mid-1800s. Historians are not sure whether the ranch's name derived from the Spanish word for "small pipe" or from an Indian word meaning "alkali flat." In the 1970s, Canutillo became a home base for owners, breeders, and trainers of horses racing at New Mexico tracks.

CANYON

Panhandle • Randall County • 12,628

Canyon's founder, Lincoln Guy Conner, settled here in late 1887. His dugout home became the location of the post office and general store. A. L. Hammond, who opened a blacksmith's shop, proposed naming the town Canyon City after the spectacular Palo Duro Canyon nearby. It was renamed Canyon in 1911.

CARBON

Central Texas • Eastland County • 287

This community originated in 1881. The engineer who platted the town-site gave the town its name, saying it was rich in minerals. He also named the streets for mineral deposits, such as Anthracite, Lignite, and Coal.

CARLSBAD

West central Texas • Tom Green County • 100

T. J. Clegg founded this North Concho River valley town in 1907, after buying the valley's Hughes Ranch. He and his partners advertised the new town, which they called Hughes, as a health resort featuring mineral water with medicinal benefits. Residents decided in 1908 to rename the town Carlsbad, after a famed spa in central Europe. Four years later, state health officers opened a large tuberculosis sanitorium here.

CARMINE

Central Texas • Fayette County • 224 • kahr-MEEN

Dr. Benjamin J. Thigpen moved here in late 1883, platted the site for this town, and named it Sylvan. It was renamed Carmean in 1886 in honor of John Carmean, a pioneer resident of the area. Because the similarity between Carmean and the name of another town, Cameron, caused much mail to be missent, postal officials changed the spelling to Carmine in 1892. Residents did not change their pronunciation of the name, however.

CARRIZO SPRINGS
Southwest Texas • Dimmit County • 5,781 • kuh-REE-zoh SPRINGZ

Frontiersman Levi English founded Carrizo Springs in the 1860s, leading some 400 people from Atascosa County to settle here. The town was named for carrizo, a cane grass growing in abundance around the area's numerous springs.

CARROLLTON
North central Texas • Dallas County • 97,950

There are at least eight other U.S. towns named Carrollton, and some historians believe that this Carrollton was named by early settlers who came from one, or possibly even two, of the others. Or Carrollton may be the namesake of Daniel Joseph Carroll, an Englishman who arrived as a member of the Peters Colony. William S. Peters established the colony in 1841 on a land grant received from the Republic of Texas.

CARTHAGE
Louisiana border • Panola County • 6,631

Carthage was established as the Panola County seat in 1848. An early settler donated 100 acres for the townsite, and state legislator Spearman Holland named it for Carthage, Mississippi, his home town. Two natives of small rural communities south of Carthage became internationally famous a century later: country music stars Tex Ritter, born at Murvaul, and Jim Reeves, born at Galloway.

CASTROVILLE
Southwest Texas • Medina County • 2,714

Land agent Henri Castro brought emigrants from France and Alsace to this location on the Medina River in 1844. The town they established was named Castroville in his honor. Castro designed the town like a European village in which individual farm plots surrounded small town lots.

CAT SPRING
Southeast Texas • Austin County • 76

Robert Kleberg and Ludwig Von Roeder led a group of German immigrants who settled here in 1834. Von Roeder's son, Leopold, slew a puma at one of the springs near his home; the incident gave the town its name.

CEDAR HILL
North central Texas • Dallas and Ellis counties • 28,000

Founded in the 1850s, this town was named for the cedars growing here in the rolling hills south of Dallas. Townspeople rebuilt their community after an 1856 tornado claimed nine lives and blew away almost everything. Cedar Hill remained primarily a farming trade center well into the twentieth century, but population ascended swiftly beginning in the late 1970s as homebuilders moved into Dallas' southern suburbs.

CEDAR PARK
Central Texas • Williamson County • 11,434

George and Harriet Cluck's ranch was the center of a settlement called Running Brushy that developed here in the 1870s. The Austin & Northwestern Railroad crossed the ranch in 1882, and the railroad changed the community's name to Brueggerhoff after the partner of a company official. Emmett Cluck, son of the ranch owners, became postmaster in 1892 and renamed the town Cedar Park. For many years production of cedar posts was an important part of the town's economy.

CEE VEE
Northwest Texas • Cottle County • 45

When Will Newsom applied for a post office to be established at this townsite on former CV Ranch land, he expected the name to be CV. Instead, postal officials spelled it out as Cee Vee. The office opened in 1929, and Newsom served as postmaster until the 1940s.

CELINA
North central Texas • Collin County • 2,060 • suh-LYE-nuh

Celina, founded in 1879, was named by John Mulkey for Celina, Tennessee, his home town. The community moved a mile in 1902 to a new townsite on the Red River, Texas & Southern Railway.

CENTER
Louisiana border • Shelby County • 5,024

Center, named for its central location in Shelby County, originated around 1856 when three area residents donated land for the development of a town. Ten years later, the citizens of Shelby County voted to make Center the new county seat. A post office opened in 1866 and the town incorporated in 1895.

CHANNELVIEW
Southeast Texas • Harris County • 28,823

This industrial suburb was named in 1933 for its location on the Houston Ship Channel. Previously it had been known as Cedar Bluff, Old River, and Arcadia.

CHANNING
Panhandle • Hartley County • 284

Channing was originally the headquarters of the immense XIT Ranch. The town was named for Channing Rivers, paymaster of the Fort Worth

Cowboys of the XIT Ranch, 1896. Courtesy of the Panhandle-Plains Historical Museum.

& Denver City Railroad, when the rail line was extended through this area. In a 1903 election, voters decided that Channing would replace Hartley as the county seat, so XIT cowboys went to Hartley, mounted the wooden county courthouse on wheels, and moved it to Channing.

CHARLOTTE
South Texas • Atascosa County • 1,609

Real estate developer Charles F. Simmons named Charlotte and two other Atascosa County towns, Christine and Imogene, for his daughters. Charlotte was laid out in 1910 in the shape of a wagon wheel. Its streets spread out like spokes from the central business area.

CHEROKEE
Central Texas • San Saba County • 175 • CHER-uh-kee

This town, founded in 1878, was named for nearby Cherokee Creek, which took its name either for a settler's Cherokee wife or for an 1839 battle between frontiersmen and Cherokee Indians.

CHESTER
Southeast Texas • Tyler County • 332

When the Missouri-Kansas-Texas Railroad built a rail line through Tyler County in 1883, lots along the route were put up for sale. Residents of nearby Peach Tree Village moved to Chester, the new town. It was named for Chester Arthur, who became president after James Garfield was assassinated in 1880.

CHILDRESS
Panhandle • Childress County • 5,197

The fledgling communities of Childress City and Henry consolidated in the 1880s to become the town of Childress, seat of Childress County. Both were named for George Campbell Childress, author of the Texas Declaration of Independence.

CHILLICOTHE
Oklahoma border • Hardeman County • 803 • chil-ih-KAH-thih

Settler Ed Jones, who migrated to Texas around 1886, named this community for Chillicothe, Missouri. The name, according to one source, is a Shawnee word meaning "the big town where we live."

CHINA
Southeast Texas • Jefferson County • 1,198

An 1860s water stop on the Texas & New Orleans Railway was called China Grove because of an adjacent grove of chinaberry trees. The railroad later designated its depot as China, and the town that grew up here took the same name.

CHINA GROVE
South Texas • Bexar County • 1,211

At various times in Texas history, other small towns named China Grove—for local groves of chinaberry trees—have appeared and then disappeared or have been renamed. This village, on the other hand, was immortalized in the 1973 Doobie Brothers song "China Grove," about the residents of a "sleepy little town/down around San Antone." By the mid-1990s, the town was less sleepy as it began to participate in the San Antonio area's growth.

CHIRENO
East Texas • Nacogdoches County • 518 • shuh-REE-noh

Jose Antonio Chireno was one of the pioneers who settled on the Texas frontier in 1790 after receiving land grants from the government of Spain. Dr. John Newton Fall came to Texas from Georgia, acquired some land from Jose Chireno, and began developing a town named for him.

CHRISTOVAL
West central Texas • Tom Green County • 216 • kris-TOH-v'l

Local historians are divided over the origin of Christoval's name. One version holds that it is a shortened form of Christ's Valley; the more widely accepted version attributes it to Christopher Columbus Doty, a merchant who applied to open a post office here. After the first name he proposed was rejected, Doty suggested Christobal (the Spanish equivalent of Christopher). Postal officials approved the name, with slightly altered spelling, in 1889 and appointed Doty postmaster.

CIBOLO
South central Texas • Guadalupe County • 1,996 • SEE-buh-loh

This town grew up along Cibolo Creek in the 1870s and 1880s. According to local lore, the creek was given its name—the Spanish word for "buffalo"—because Indians stampeded herds of buffalo over the creek's steep banks, disabling the animals so they could be killed for hides and winter food.

CIRCLE BACK
New Mexico border • Bailey County • 10

In the 1940s, Circle Back was a community of 150 consisting of a general store, gasoline station, and grade school attended by children from the surrounding ranching area. The community was named for a ranch where cattle were branded with circles on their backs. Its population dwindled to a single family of four by the 1980s but increased to 10 residents in 1990.

CISCO
Central Texas • Eastland County • 4,165 • SIS-koh

John Cisco, a New York banker, was involved in financing the Texas Central Railroad. The Texas Central's tracks crossed those of the Texas & Pacific Railway line here in 1881. A settlement called Red Gap moved to the railway junction and took the name Cisco in 1884. The Eastland County oil boom of 1919-21 boosted Cisco's population to 15,000 and above. One of those arriving in 1919 was young Conrad Hilton. He came to Cisco hoping to buy a small bank but was unsuccessful. Looking for a place to stay the night, he went to the town's Mobley Hotel and heard the hotel clerk shout "Full up!" to a lobby full of men clamoring to rent beds in eight-hour shifts. "They were acting like sardines trying to get into a can," Hilton later related. He altered his plan, bought the Mobley Hotel, and after examining its books, decided it was a gold mine—or, as he described it to a friend, "a cross between a flophouse and a gold mine." The Mobley was the first link in what became the far-flung Hilton hotel empire.

CLARENDON
Panhandle • Donley County • 2,196 • KLAIR-in-duhn

Lewis H. Carhart, a circuit-riding Methodist minister who sought to establish a utopian community of devout, educated Christians, founded Clarendon in 1878. He named it in honor of his wife, the former Clara Sully. The colony attracted a wider variety of settlers than Carhart anticipated, and in 1880 he left for Dallas.

CLARKSVILLE

Northeast Texas • Red River County • 4,397

Clarksville, the Red River County seat, was named for its founder, James Clark, who settled near here in 1826. His fellow settlers, believing

The Red River County courthouse in Clarksville. Courtesy of Ray Miller.

the area was part of the Louisiana Purchase, were so convinced they were living in the United States that they sent Clark to the Arkansas legislature from 1827 to 1832. From the 1840s until the Civil War, the town was the most important trading center in northeast Texas, receiving goods from New Orleans via steamboats on the Red River.

CLEBURNE
Central Texas • Johnson County • 24,037

This town was founded in 1867 as the new Johnson County seat. It took its name for Patrick R. Cleburne, a Confederate Army general killed in combat.

CLEVELAND
Southeast Texas • Liberty County • 8,215

Cleveland developed on a 63.3-acre tract deeded to the Houston, East & West Texas Railway by landowner Charles Lander Cleveland in 1878. The town became a lumber shipping point, and a century later began to share in the growth of metropolitan Houston.

CLIFTON
Central Texas • Bosque County • 3,648

Settlers arriving here in the early 1850s called their community Cliff Town, for the area's impressive limestone cliffs. The name eventually evolved into Clifton.

CLUTE
Gulf Coast • Brazoria County • 10,422

Clute, also known as Clute City, was named for John Clute, a partial owner of the plantation land on which the town developed in the 1940s.

CLYDE
West central Texas • Callahan County • 3,222

Robert Clyde was foreman of the construction gang based at a camp here while building the Texas & Pacific Railway. A post office opened at "Camp Clyde" in June 1881. The town grew steadily, adding several churches and stores by the early 1900s.

Coahoma

West Texas • Howard County • 1,315 • koh-HOH-muh

Coahoma takes its name from an Indian word meaning "signal," referring to a small hill nearby that was known as a signal point for a local tribe. A settlement sprang up after this locale became a stop on the Texas & Pacific Railway in 1881.

Coleman

Central Texas • Coleman County • 5,368

Coleman was established in 1876 as the Coleman County seat. The name honored Robert M. Coleman, a native of Kentucky, who came to Texas in 1832, signed the Texas Declaration of Independence, and was aide-de-camp to General Sam Houston during the Battle of San Jacinto. Soon after its founding, the town gained a cemetery when two cowboys had a gunfight in front of one of the general stores.

Collegeport

Gulf Coast • Matagorda County • 91

When the Hurd Land Company began promoting this town in 1908, it promised to establish a Gulf Coast University of Industrial Arts here. The town post office derived its name from this expectation, but the promoters' promises were never fulfilled and Collegeport remained a community of fewer than 100 residents.

College Station

Southeast Texas • Brazos County • 62,993

This town, home of the Agricultural & Mechanical College of Texas, adopted its name in the 1870s. Ninety years later, there was an unsuccessful attempt to change the name because Texas A&M had become a university.

Colleyville

North central Texas • Tarrant County • 18,100

Residents of this town, which developed as a cluster of rural communities in the late 1800s, decided in 1915 to name their town for Dr. Howard Colley, who practiced medicine in the area for 40 years. After the mid-1960s, Colleyville's growth was stimulated by the northward spread of metropolitan Fort Worth and by construction and expansion of Dallas-Fort Worth Airport.

COLLINSVILLE
Oklahoma border • Grayson County • 1,206

Two rural communities, Springville and Toadsuck, existed here before the Civil War. After the war, Mrs. L. M. Collins came to Springville from Ann Arbor, Michigan, and organized what may have been the first free school in North Texas. In the early 1890s, citizens voted to incorporate the combined town and rename it in honor of Mrs. Collins.

COLMESNEIL
Southeast Texas • Tyler County • 625 • KOHLMS-neel

In 1884, the Missouri-Kansas-Texas Railroad and Texas & New Orleans tracks intersected here to create a railroad center for Tyler County. The town that sprung up at the intersection was named for W. T. Colmesneil, a railroad conductor.

COLORADO CITY
West Texas • Mitchell County • 6,040

Colorado City, the "Mother City of West Texas," is the oldest town between El Paso and Weatherford. It began in 1877 as a Texas Ranger camp on the Colorado River. After the Texas & Pacific Railway established a station here in 1881, the town quickly became a cattle-shipping point for a vast region of Texas, and its stores and saloons prospered.

COLUMBUS
Southeast Texas • Colorado County • 3,763

Settled in 1823 by members of Stephen F. Austin's colony, this town is said to have been first named Beeson's Ferry for Benjamin Beeson, who operated a ferry on the Colorado River. It was renamed Columbus in 1835, reportedly at the suggestion of a former resident of Columbus, Ohio. When Colorado County organized in 1836, Columbus became the county seat.

COMANCHE

Central Texas • Comanche County • 4,503 • kuh-MANN-chee

This town was established in 1858 as the Comanche County seat. Both the county and the town took their names from the Comanche Indians, who dominated this area in the eighteenth and early nineteenth centuries.

COMBES

Far south Texas • Cameron County • 2,631

Combes was named for Dr. Joe Combes of Brownsville who saved the life of James H. Dishman, a prominent farmer, rancher, and mill operator, after a cattle rustler shot and gravely wounded him.

COMFORT

South central Texas • Kendall County • 1,750

German pioneers who arrived here in 1854 wanted to call their new community Gemutlichkeit, a word conveying a sense of good will and tranquility, but they decided to shorten and anglicize the name to Comfort. Early merchants included Peter Joseph Ingenhuett and August Faltin. Ingenhuett's general merchandise store, established in 1867, was recognized in 1998 as Texas's oldest general store in continuous operation. Descendants of Faltin still carried on his retail business, begun in 1879.

COMMERCE

Northeast Texas • Hunt County • 7,125

Pioneer merchant William Jernigan gave Commerce, established in 1853, its name. He said he hoped and expected this new town would become a commercial center. There were 18 businesses in town, including a wagon factory, when Commerce incorporated in 1885. Two railroad lines and a bank soon followed.

CONCAN

Southwest Texas • Uvalde County • 225

Concan derived its name from a Mexican card game played in this little settlement during the mid-nineteenth century, under the large oak and cypress trees lining the banks of the Frio River.

CONROE

Southeast Texas • Montgomery County • 40,686

Isaac Conroe, a Houston lumberman, operated a sawmill in this vicinity in the 1880s, first at Stewarts Creek and later at a junction of the International & Great Northern rail line. When a post office opened in the sawmill's commissary in 1884, it took the name Conroe's Switch, later shortened to Conroe. Conroe became a major shipping point for livestock, lumber, cotton, and other products, and wildcatter George Strake's discovery of the Conroe oil field in December 1931 bolstered the economy during the Great Depression.

CONVERSE

South Texas • Bexar County • 10,773

This community of German farmers, located on the Galveston, Harrisburg & San Antonio Railway, was named for James Converse, the railroad's chief engineer. Although Converse's population was under 300 at mid-century, the town emerged as a fast-growing San Antonio suburb in the 1980s.

COOPER

Northeast Texas • Delta County • 2,173

This town, founded in 1870, was named for State Senator L. W. Cooper, who played a key role in the creation of Delta County and in the designation of Cooper as its county seat.

COPPELL

North central Texas • Dallas and Denton counties • 29,000 • kah-PEL

At its establishment in 1887, the post office here took the name Gibbs Station, in honor of Barnett Gibbs, elected lieutenant governor of Texas in 1884. In 1892, the name changed to Coppell, for George A. Coppell, a railroad employee and early settler. From 1925 to 1950, the town's population was estimated at 200, but in the last half of the century, Coppell became a full-fledged Metroplex suburb.

COPPERAS COVE
Central Texas • Coryell County • 29,515 • kahp-ruhs KOHV

Marsden Ogletree, appointed postmaster of Copperas Cove in 1879, established the post office near a spring in the cove of a large hill. The name he selected refers to the coppery taste of the spring water. The Gulf, Colorado & Santa Fe Railway's arrival in 1882 made the community a busy shipping point. Records show that Copperas Cove shipments in the month of January 1909 included 136 freight cars loaded with cattle, 35 cars of cottonseed, 5,500 bales of cotton, 3 cars of turkeys, and 1,000 cases of eggs.

CORPUS CHRISTI
Gulf Coast • Nueces County • 275,762

This small village became known in the 1840s as Corpus Christi ("the body of Christ"), the same name bestowed upon its bay by the first European to visit this area. Spanish explorer Alonso Alvarez de Pineda sailed into the bay on the religious feast day of Corpus Christi in 1519, and chose its name accordingly. Although it became the county seat in 1846, the town grew slowly until the 1870s, when Corpus Christi began to benefit from booming markets in wool and cattle, and from railroad and seaport traffic.

CORRIGAN
Southeast Texas • Polk County • 2,268

Corrigan developed as two railroads constructed their tracks through this area. The Houston, East & West Texas Railway came first, in 1881, and the Trinity & Sabine Railway arrived in 1882. Early settlers named the community in honor of Pat Corrigan, conductor of the first passenger train to stop here. The conductor's grandson, Galveston native Douglas Corrigan, made news more than a half century later with his "wrong-way" solo transatlantic flight to Ireland.

CORSICANA
East central Texas • Navarro County • 24,168

At its founding in 1848, this county seat drew its name from the island of Corsica, birthplace of Jose Antonio Navarro's father. Navarro was the

Jose Antonio Navarro. Courtesy of Houston Metropolitan Research Center, Houston Public Library.

Texas revolutionary hero for whom Navarro County was named. In 1895, while drilling a well for artesian water, a local company found a large pocket of oil, later described as the first significant oil find west of the Mississippi River.

Cost

South central Texas • Gonzales County • 62

This community, only a mile from the site of the opening battle of the Texas Revolution, was first called Oso by German settlers arriving in the 1880s. In 1897 postal officials rejected Oso as a name for the town post office. For unexplained reasons, they substituted the name Cost instead.

Cotulla

South Texas • La Salle County • 4,293 • kuh-TOO-luh

Joe Cotulla, a Polish immigrant, founded this town in 1881. He offered 120 acres of land to induce the International & Great Northern Railroad to extend its tracks to a townsite here. The railroad accepted Cotulla's offer, and used part of the land as a depot site. Construction began on other townsite lots in 1882, and in 1883 voters chose Cotulla as the county seat. After several years in which gunfights were rather frequent—and fatal—the town became more peaceful.

Crane

West Texas • Crane County • 3,453

Crane and its county were named for William Carey Crane, a Baptist minister who served as president of Baylor University for 22 years until his death in 1885. He was the first president of the Texas State Teachers Association, a biographer of Sam Houston, and a leader in reorganizing the Texas public school system after the Civil War and Reconstruction. Although Crane County was formed in 1887, its settlers numbered only a few dozen until a major new oil field was discovered here in 1926. Crane became an instant boomtown consisting of some simple wooden buildings and hundreds of tents. O. M. Kimmison, who opened a real estate office, laid out a townsite and named the streets for his sons and daughters. He also invited a preacher to come to Crane and hold church services. According to a local historian, gamblers viewed the invitation with such hostility they gave Kimmison a beating. Crane County still relies on oil and gas production and cattle ranching, and Crane remains its only town.

CROCKETT

East Texas • Houston County • 6,902

Crockett, incorporated in 1837, was named for David Crockett, the legendary frontiersman who died at the Alamo. Andrew Edward Gossett, who donated land for development of the county seat, and his father, Elijah, selected the name. Crockett's post office opened in 1838, and a courthouse was constructed in the same year.

CROSBY

Southeast Texas • Harris County • 2,233

This town in eastern Harris County is reputed to have been known as Lick Skillet at one time. In the late 1860s, it was named for a railroad construction manager, G. I. Crosby. The first store opened in 1865 and the community began to grow, acquiring a post office in 1877.

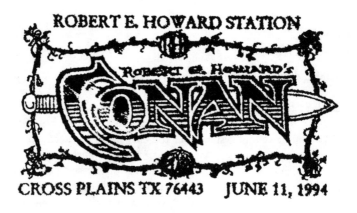

CROSS PLAINS

West central Texas • Callahan County • 1,021

Settlers decided to name this community for its location at a point on the West Texas plains crossed by cattle trails, horse traders, circuit-riding preachers, and trappers. Previously, the settlement had been called Turkey Creek. The town grew from 25 residents to 175 by 1885 and acquired a cotton gin, wagonmaker, gristmill, and general store. It was later home to Robert E. Howard, the fantasy writer who created Conan the Barbarian.

CROWLEY

North central Texas • Tarrant County • 7,350 • KROU-ley

The Gulf, Colorado & Santa Fe rail line arrived here in 1885. Grateful for access to the railroad, citizens relocated their homes to be nearer to the tracks. They also named their town in honor of S. H. Crowley, master of transportation for the railroad company.

CRYSTAL CITY

Southwest Texas • Zavala County • 8,197

Pioneer settlers termed water from this area's artesian wells "as clear as crystal," and land developers Carl Groos and E. J. Buckingham drew on the phrase when they named this town in 1907. In 1909, the Crystal City & Uvalde Railroad began constructing tracks connecting Crystal City with Uvalde, Carrizo Springs, and Gardendale. With rail transportation available, Crystal City quickly became a center for shipping the spinach, carrots, peppers, onions, and other vegetables grown in great quantities on surrounding farms, and Del Monte and other companies later established canning plants here.

CUERO

South Texas • DeWitt County • 6,913 • KWEHR-oh

Cuero's name, a Spanish noun translated as "rawhide" or "leather," came from Cuero Creek, four miles north of this county seat. Spanish mapmakers gave the creek its name after learning that Indians recovered hides from the buffalo and other animals they found mired in the creek bottoms. The town of Cuero was established in 1873 as a stop on the new Gulf, Western Texas & Pacific rail line.

CUNEY

East Texas • Cherokee County • 187 • KYOO-nee

In an area settled by former slaves soon after the Civil War, the village of Cuney developed as a flag stop on the Texas & New Orleans Railroad around 1902. H. L. Price, a Palestine bank officer, and several other investors platted a townsite in 1914. The town was named for Price's son Cuney, who was himself named for Norris W. Cuney of Galveston, a black city council member who led the Republican Party in Texas during the 1880s and 1890s.

CUT AND SHOOT
Southeast Texas • Montgomery County • 1,400

Cut and Shoot traces its peculiar name to a disagreement between two factions in the community during the summer of 1912. Baptist and Methodist citizens had jointly constructed a building to serve as the community's schoolhouse and church, with the understanding that Mormons and Apostolic Pentecostals would be barred from using it. According to county historian W. H. Gandy, someone gave an Apostolic minister named Stamps permission to preach there, and a confrontation ensued between those who arrived to hear Stamps and others who had locked the building to prevent him from speaking. Many involved in the confrontation were armed with knives and guns, and, Gandy relates, during the heated exchange a young boy shouted, "I'm scared—I'm going to cut around the corner and shoot through the bushes." Actually, no cutting or shooting took place, but the leaders of the two factions filed charges against one another. A judge in Conroe ordered both men to pay fines. Despite the absence of bloodshed, the town became known as Cut and Shoot, "the place where they had the cuttin' and shootin' fracas."

DAINGERFIELD
Northeast Texas • Morris County • 2,779

London Daingerfield was killed in 1830 while leading about 100 men in a fight with Indians in this vicinity. The town named after him originated in the early 1840s. In the Civil War years, three tanyards opened here to make leather for Confederate soldiers' boots, shoes, and saddles. Daingerfield became the seat of Morris County in 1875, the same year that the East Line & Red River Railroad built its tracks a half mile from the town. After a destructive fire in 1879, most of the town's businesses relocated to the railroad.

DAISETTA
Southeast Texas • Liberty County • 1,027

Daisetta was founded after the discovery of the Hull oil field in this area near the end of World War I. A post office opened in 1921 with a name proposed by Newt Farris, proprietor of one of the town's first stores, that combined the first names of Daisy Barrett and Etta White. This town is connected with neighboring Hull by a long business street, and the two are often called Hull-Daisetta.

DALHART
Panhandle • Dallam and Hartley counties • 6,535

In 1901, when the Chicago, Rock Island & Mexico rail line crossed the Fort Worth & Denver City tracks near the boundary of Dallam and Hartley counties, a settlement sprang up at the junction. Postal officials accepted the name Dalhart—a combination of the first syllables of the county names—for the town's post office.

DALLAS
North central Texas • Dallas County • 1,052,300

In 1843 Dallas' first settler, John Neely Bryan, established a trading post at the three forks of the Trinity River. There was a cluster of other cabins around Bryan's home, along with a general store and a two-room tavern. The number of settlers was sufficient for the Republic of Texas to begin

John Neely Bryan's cabin in Dallas. Courtesy of Houston Metropolitan Research Center, Houston Public Library.

postal service to the town, and Bryan was appointed postmaster. He said he was naming the post office "for my friend Dallas" but never indicated whom, among the several people he knew named Dallas, he had in mind. Fewer than 800 people lived in Dallas when the Civil War ended, but phenomenal growth came in the 1870s with the arrival of railroads, bankers, retail merchants, wholesalers, lumber dealers, builders, and hotel operators. The *Dallas Morning News* began publishing in 1885, and the State Fair of Texas was organized in 1887. The census of 1890 revealed that Dallas, with 38,067 residents, was the most populous town in Texas.

DANEVANG
Southeast Texas • Wharton County • 61 • DAN-uh-vang

The Dansk Folkesamfund founded this community in 1894 as a Danish colony, for the purpose of preserving the language and culture of the Danes in the Southwest. The folk society obtained 25,000 acres for settlers, and during the first year about 70 families arrived to begin the settlement named Danevang, or "Danish meadow."

DAVILLA
East central Texas • Milam County • 200 • duh-VIHL-uh

Named for Miguel Davila (with an erroneous spelling of his name), this town began when a surveyor bought land from Davila's estate, platted a townsite, and sold lots. In 1871, the Davilla post office opened.

DAWN
Panhandle • Deaf Smith County • 52

J. H. Parrish moved into a dugout home in this vicinity in 1889 and soon afterward opened a general store for the area's ranchers. Parish named his store "The Dawn of Civilization," and some sources say the town derived its name from the store, while others contend it came from an exclamation by Parrish upon his arrival here, "This is the dawn of a new day!

DAYTON
Southeast Texas • Liberty County • 5,964

From the 1830s until the mid-1850s, this town was called West Liberty and was considered part of Liberty, the county seat. Liberty was on the east bank of the Trinity River and West Liberty on the west bank, with a road and a ferry connecting the two. Around 1855, some began to call

West Liberty Day's Town and Dayton Station after landowner I. C. Day, who came here from Tennessee in 1830. The local post office was established with the name Dayton in 1877, although the town officially remained West Liberty until the mid-1880s.

DECATUR
North Texas • Wise County • 4,770

When the Texas Legislature created Wise County in 1856, Decatur was founded and designated as the county seat. Most legislators expected the town to be named Taylorsville to honor General Zachary Taylor. But Absalom Bishop, a legislator who resided in Wise County, vehemently opposed the general's affiliation with the Whig Party. He arranged instead for the county seat to be named in honor of Commodore Stephen Decatur, who fought at Tripoli and in the War of 1812.

DEER PARK
Southeast Texas • Harris County • 30,873

Deer Park derived its name from a private park for deer that once occupied this townsite. A small community developed after the Galveston, Harrisburg & San Antonio Railway established a station here in 1892. Following World War II, extensive industrial development began in this area along the Houston Ship Channel. The town's population has increased forty-fold since 1950.

DE KALB
Arkansas border • Bowie County • 1,954 • dih KAB

De Kalb was first settled in the mid-1830s and named for Major General Johann Kalb (Baron de Kalb), an American Revolutionary War hero. Legendary frontiersman David Crockett, who stopped here on his way to join Sam Houston's Texas army in its fight for independence from Mexico, is said to have suggested the name to local residents.

DELL CITY
Far west Texas • Hudspeth County • 711

Dell City originated in 1948, when irrigated farms were established in this fertile valley after the discovery of vast pools of underground water. The town's post office opened in 1949 and took its name from the song "The Farmer in the Dell."

DELMITA
Far south Texas • Starr County • 50 • del-MEET-uh

Niceforo G. Pena, Sr., founded this rural hamlet in 1919, naming it Zaragosa. Because of confusion with mail addressed to Saragosa in Reeves County, postal officials asked Pena to submit a new name in 1931. Pena asked each of his seven sons to draw a letter of the alphabet and then combined the seven letters to produce the name Delmita.

DEL RIO
Southwest Texas • Val Verde County • 34,431

Del Rio owes its origin to the San Felipe Agricultural, Manufacturing & Irrigation Company, which bought several thousand acres of land along San Felipe Creek in 1869, completed an irrigation-canal network in 1871, and began selling small tracts of rich farmland to new settlers. The town of truck farmers and their families was first referred to as San Felipe del Rio—a name Spanish missionaries had given this area when they arrived here on St. Philip's Day in 1635, according to local legend. Postal officials shortened the name to Del Rio in 1883 to avoid further confusion with the San Felipe post office in Austin County.

DENISON
Oklahoma border • Grayson County • 22,076

Expecting the Missouri-Kansas-Texas Railroad—nicknamed "the Katy"—to route its tracks through this area, William B. Munson, Sr., and R. S. Stevens bought land here and had it divided into town lots sold at public auction in 1872. The town was named for George Denison, the Katy's vice president. President Dwight D. Eisenhower was born in Denison in 1890.

DENTON
North central Texas • Denton County • 73,050

Denton, like its county, was named in honor of John B. Denton, a lawyer, itinerant Methodist minister, and captain in the Republic of Texas army who was fatally shot during a fight with Indians at the 1841 battle of Village Creek. Founded in 1857, Denton replaced Alton as the county seat. Two railroads—the Texas & Pacific and the Missouri-Kansas-Texas lines—arrived in 1881. Even more important for the town's future was the founding of North Texas Normal College (now the University of North Texas) in 1890 and the Girls' Industrial College (now Texas Woman's University) in 1903.

DENVER CITY
New Mexico border • Yoakum County • 5,063

After discovery of the Wasson oil field, E. S. Ameen and Ben Eggink laid out a town they named Wasson in Gaines County in 1935. When it appeared in 1939 that the field's major producing wells would be across the county line, in Yoakum County, the two men decided to transplant the town closer to the wells. To encourage early residents of Wasson to move, they donated land to the Methodist church. Since opposition remained, they transported the buildings on a Sunday morning, apparently calculating that the townspeople would be in church and that, when they discovered what was happening, they would not be able to obtain a court order that day to prevent it. Ameen and Eggink named the new townsite Denver City, because the Denver Producing & Refining Company had opened the new pool in Yoakum County.

DESDEMONA
Central Texas • Eastland County • 180

Desdemona, developed in the 1870s, was named for the daughter of a local justice of the peace. The town experienced an oil boom between 1918 and 1923, but thereafter population fell so sharply that the town government was dissolved in 1936.

DESOTO
North central Texas • Dallas County • 36,600

Four families settled this community in the southern part of Dallas County in the early 1840s. When a post office was opened in 1884, it was named DeSoto, either for a local resident, Dr. Thomas Hernando DeSoto Stewart, or for the sixteenth-century Spanish explorer Hernando de Soto.

DEVINE
Southwest Texas • Medina County • 4,749

Devine, founded in 1881 on the International & Great Northern Railroad, was named for Thomas Jefferson Devine, a native of Halifax, Nova Scotia, who came to Texas in 1843 as a young lawyer and began a distinguished career as a jurist.

DEWEYVILLE
Louisiana border • Newton County • 1,324 • DOO-ih-vil

Deweyville began in 1898 as a settlement adjacent to the Sabine Tram Company sawmill built at a Sabine River crossing called Possum Bluff. The town name honored Admiral George Dewey, who led the U.S. Navy to victory that year in the battle of Manila Bay.

D'HANIS
Southwest Texas • Medina County • 548 • duh-HAY-niss

D'Hanis was the last of four villages established by Henri Castro, who had received a contract from the Republic of Texas to recruit colonists from Europe to settle on the Texas frontier. A group of 29 Alsatian families arrived at this location in 1847 and received 20-acre farm tracts along with their town lots. Castro named the town for his Antwerp colonization manager, William D'Hanis.

DIBOLL
East Texas • Angelina County • 5,367 • DYE-bawl

J. C. Diboll sold 7,000 acres of virgin pine and hardwood in 1893 to Thomas Lewis Latane Temple, who founded the Southern Pine Lumber Company here and built a sawmill. More settlers arrived as sawmill operations began, and a school and post office both opened in 1894. Diboll, headquarters for the vast Temple-Inland forest products empire begun by Temple, remained a company town until the 1950s.

DICKINSON
Gulf Coast • Galveston County • 17,777

Pioneer settlers arrived here during the Republic of Texas era. Like the local bayou, the town was named for John Dickinson, one of Stephen F. Austin's "Old 300" colonists, who received a land grant in this vicinity.

DIME BOX
Central Texas • Lee County • 313

The town of Dime Box originated in the 1870s as a settlement around Joseph Brown's sawmill. Until a post office was established in 1877, a small box at the mill served as a mailbox for area residents. They placed dimes in the box to compensate John W. Ratliff, the horse rider who made a weekly delivery of mail from the post office at Giddings.

DIMMITT
Panhandle • Castro County • 4,107

Dimmitt was established in 1890 near the center of Castro County by the Bedford Town & Land Development Company. Hilory G. Bedford, president of the company, handled the sale of lots at the townsite. He named the town in honor of his wife's uncle W. C. Dimmitt, a minister from Kentucky and one of the company's investors.

DINERO
South Texas • Live Oak County • 344 • dee-NEH-roh

The community that started growing here in the 1840s was first known as Barlow's Ferry, after a ferry operator on the Nueces River. Dinero, the Spanish word for "money," became the town name after rumors of buried treasure brought Mexican fortune-seekers here in 1872.

DING DONG
Central Texas • Bell County • 225

C. C. "Cohn" Hoover, a farmer with artistic talent, gave this Bell County settlement its name in 1923 when he painted a sign for the newly built general store. Cousins Bert Bell and Z. O. Bell, the proprietors, accepted Hoover's offer to paint the sign at no charge if allowed to design it himself. The sign pictured two large bells emblazoned with the initials of the cousins, and Hoover surprised them by providing a name for their store, lettering "Ding Dong" between the two bells. The community gave Ding Dong a ringing endorsement by readily adopting the store's name as its own. In the 1990s, Ding Dong gained the 777 Estates residential subdivision, several businesses, and a volunteer fire department.

DODSON
Panhandle • Collingsworth County • 117

Rancher Elmore Dodson, tired of traveling three or four days by wagon to buy groceries and other supplies at Quanah, decided to use part of his horse pasture as the site of a new town. In 1910 he donated 200 acres to the Wichita Falls & Northwestern Railway (later bought by the Missouri-Kansas-Texas line). The railroad extended its tracks through Dodson's ranch, established a station called Dodsonville, and brought a trainload of Oklahomans to a community celebration launching the town. In the 1920s, the town incorporated and shortened its name to Dodson.

DOMINO
Northeast Texas • Cass County • 105

The Texas Pacific Railway established a flag stop, originally called Alamo Mills, at this location in the late nineteenth century, attracting settlers who soon formed a community. A local historian ascribes the new name to residents' penchant for playing dominoes at the train stop during their leisure hours. The practice led rail travelers to call the community Domino.

DONIE
East central Texas • Freestone County • 206 • DOH-nih

In 1905 residents sent an application for a town post office to Washington. The name they proposed—that of the man who founded the community in the nineteenth century, but historians disagree whether it was Dovie or Douie or Dewey—was misread as Donie.

DONNA
Far south Texas • Hidalgo County • 15,437

In 1904 the new St. Louis, Brownsville & Mexico Railway line reached this location, attracting settlers who soon formed a community. A depot built in 1907 was named Donna in honor of Donna Hooks Fletcher, whose father, T. J. Hooks, was a pioneer landowner. In 1908, when the Donna post office opened, Mrs. Fletcher was appointed postmaster.

DOUGLASS
East Texas • Nacogdoches County • 75

Douglass was founded in 1836 and named for Kelsey Harris Douglass, who established several businesses here. Douglass represented Nacogdoches County in the Republic of Texas congress in 1837 and 1838. The next year, he led 500 Texas troops who routed Chief Duwali's Cherokee army in the Battle of the Neches.

DRIFTWOOD
South central Texas • Hays County • 21

This nineteenth-century inland settlement, far from the Gulf of Mexico and other shores, was named for the volume of twigs and tree branches floating along a nearby creek.

DUBLIN
North central Texas • Erath County • 3,622

Although it's been asserted that Dublin was named for the capital of Ireland, local historians contend that the name was once spelled Doublin and came from a traditional warning shouted when Indian raiders appeared, "Double in!"—a signal to move to the homes easiest to defend.

DUMAS
Panhandle • Moore County • 14,234

Anticipating the organization of Moore County in 1892, Louis Dumas and his business associates organized the Moore County Townsite Company one year earlier and bought land in the area. They platted a townsite, named it for company president Dumas, applied for a post office, and erected a hotel and general store. When the county was organized, Dumas became the county seat.

DUNCANVILLE
North central Texas • Dallas County • 36,150

Although some settlers arrived in this area as early as the 1840s, Duncanville was founded when the Chicago, Texas & Mexican Central Railroad established a rail switch here in 1880. The railroad named the location Duncan Switch after a line foreman. Postmaster Charles Nance changed the name to Duncanville in 1882.

EAGLE PASS
Southwest Texas • Maverick County • 26,141

During the U.S. war with Mexico, a border observation post here was named El Paso del Aguila (Eagle Pass) by Texas volunteers who frequently saw eagles in the area. After Fort Duncan was established two miles away in 1849, Anglo settlers moved here, and landowner John Twohig established a townsite he called Eagle Pass.

EARTH
Northwest Texas • Lamb County • 1,349

Earth began as a settlement on W. E. Halsell's ranch and acquired a post office in 1925. Postal officials in Washington rejected proposals to name the post office Fairleen or Tulsa. Halsell is said to have then submitted the name Good Earth, which postal officials shortened to Earth. According to another version of the story, a dust storm blew up at the very time villagers gathered to determine what to call their town, and they were inspired by the windblown soil.

EAST BERNARD
Southeast Texas • Wharton County • 1,706

This community was originally located on the east side of the San Bernard River. The Buffalo Bayou, Brazos & Colorado railroad depot moved from the east to the west bank in 1869, and the town and its post office moved with it. No one sought to change the name to reflect the new location, so it remains East Bernard.

EASTLAND
Central Texas • Eastland County • 3,818

Like its county, this county seat was named for Captain William Mosby Eastland, a Texan executed by order of General Antonio Lopez de Santa Anna for participating in the Mier Expedition. Charles Connellee and J. S. Daugherty platted a townsite for Eastland in 1875 and helped build a stone courthouse here.

ECLETO
South Texas • Karnes County • 22 • ih-KLEE-toh

Ecleto was named for Dry Ecleto Creek, on which this hamlet is located and where its post office opened in 1921. According to a local historian, the little town was first called Cleto, said to be an Indian name. Later, the name was given a Spanish twist as El Cleto. And, finally, Anglo ranchers shortened it to Ecleto.

EDCOUCH
Far south Texas • Hidalgo County • 3,810

Edward C. Couch, a Weslaco landowner and banker, developed a townsite here in 1926. The town and its post office were given the developer's name, in abbreviated form.

EDEN
Central Texas • Concho County • 1,726

Rancher Fred Ede established this town in 1882 by dividing a 40-acre tract into townsite lots and donating land for the public square. Ede, who had brought his family to Concho County from England two years earlier, added an "n" to his last name to create the town name.

EDINBURG
Far south Texas • Hidalgo County • 41,974

Developers who established this town in 1908 as a centrally located seat for Hidalgo County named it after Judge Dennis Chapin. But Chapin became involved in a San Antonio murder, and county commissioners decided in 1911 to change the town name. They chose Edinburg, to honor the Scottish birthplace of Rio Grande Valley pioneer John Young.

EDNA
Gulf Coast • Jackson County • 6,195

Known locally as Macaroni Station, Edna originated in 1882 as a commissary town for Italian laborers constructing the New York, Texas & Mexican Railway through this area. The town was named for one of the daughters of Count Joseph Telfener, the Italian financier whose company was building the railroad. The count also named Inez, in Victoria County, after another daughter and Louise, in Wharton County, after a sister-in-law.

EGYPT
Southeast Texas • Wharton County • 26

According to legend, farms in this vicinity had a bumper crop of corn in 1834 at a time when surrounding communities experienced a crop

The old post office at Egypt. Courtesy of Ray Miller.

failure. Noting a similarity to the Old Testament story in which Egypt supplied grain when other lands suffered a drought, people began referring to this settlement as Egypt.

EL CAMPO
Southeast Texas • Wharton County • 10,793

A railroad switching point and worker's camp established here in 1882 was the forerunner of the present-day town of El Campo. Workers shared the camp with Mexican cowboys who referred to it as "el campo." It evolved into a permanent settlement with surrounding farms producing so much hay that by 1902 El Campo claimed to be the second largest hay-shipping center in the nation.

ELDORADO
Southwest Texas • Schleicher County • 2,276

In 1895 land promoter W. B. Silliman gave this town the name of Spanish America's mythical city of gold, silver, and precious gems. When Silliman offered free town lots to families from Verand, five miles away, they moved their homes and businesses to Eldorado.

ELECTRA
Oklahoma border • Wichita County • 3,463

Electra was founded in 1907 and named for Electra Waggoner, daughter of rancher William T. Waggoner, who owned almost 600,000 acres of land in this area. Waggoner and his associates launched a national advertising campaign for the new town. The campaign proved so successful that lots were oversold and the townsite had to be expanded. Population in 1910 was 1,000 and that number rapidly quintupled after a 1911 oil boom.

ELGIN
Central Texas • Bastrop County • 5,688 • EL-gin (hard "g")

Elgin was established in 1872 on the route of the new Houston & Texas Central rail line, and its post office opened a year later. The town was named in honor of Robert Morris Elgin, the railroad's surveyor and land commissioner. Along with retail stores, Elgin's early businesses included brick and broom factories. The *Elgin Courier* began publishing around 1890.

ELKHART
East Texas • Anderson County • 1,144

An Indian named Elkheart was friendly to settlers who arrived here in the 1840s. A post office named for him opened in 1850, closed in 1851, and reopened in early 1874 with the present spelling.

ELMATON
Gulf Coast • Matagorda County • 165 • el-MAYT-'n

Although its name is officially one word, this village is also known as El Maton, Spanish for "the tough fellow" or "the killer." There are legends about the origin of the town name—one involving a drunken brawl that proved fatal to several men, another concerning a railroad accident, and a third linking the name with a slaughterhouse once located in the community.

ELM MOTT
Central Texas • McLennan County • 190

Early settlers called this rural community Geneva, but it officially became Elm Mott in 1872. A mott is defined as a small cluster of trees on a prairie, and there were numerous motts of elms in the area.

EL PASO
Far west Texas • El Paso County • 592,145

The mountain pass here, called El Paso del Rio del Norte (the River Pass of the North), was used by Indians long before Spaniard Cabeza de Vaca crossed it about 1536. In the nineteenth century, it became an important gateway to the West for gold-seekers and traders, and a favored route for stage lines and railroads crossing the Rockies. In 1852, four early settlements consolidated to form the present city of El Paso, although that name was not adopted for another six years. Before the arrival of railroads in the early 1880s, El Paso was an adobe village with a population of several hundred. The railroads transformed it into a frontier boom town. By 1900, El Paso's population was about 16,000. Famous natives of El Paso include Sandra Day O'Connor, associate justice of the U.S. Supreme Court; actress Debbie Reynolds; and journalist Sam Donaldson.

ELSA
Far south Texas • Hidalgo County • 6,461

Mexican ranchers inhabited this area before 1800, and Anglo-Americans began to arrive in 1908. The townsite developed here along the Southern Pacific Railway line in 1927 was named for the wife of land developer William George.

ELYSIAN FIELDS
Northeast Texas • Harrison County • 300

Captain Edward Smith, a Virginian who brought his family to settle here around 1837, named Elysian Fields for the paradise of Greek mythology. After an earlier journey to this area, he had described its natural beauty to a friend in New Orleans who responded, "Why, you found the Elysian Fields!"

ENCINAL
South Texas • La Salle County • 644 • en-suh-NAHL

Officials of the International & Great Northern Railroad gave the name Encinal, the Spanish word for "oak grove," to this location when they noticed oak trees on the banks of nearby Chucareto Creek. After the I&GN constructed its rail line here in 1880, settlers in the vicinity moved near the railroad tracks and formed a town.

ENERGY
Central Texas • Comanche County • 65

Charlie and Will Baxter, proprietors of the general store, picked the name Energy for this rural community's post office in 1897, observing that residents were unusually energetic people.

ENNIS
Central Texas • Ellis County • 15,250

Ennis, established in 1872 as a market town on the Houston & Texas Central Railway, was named for Colonel Cornelius Ennis, an official of the railroad. From 300 inhabitants in 1874, the population reached 3,000 in 1890. Two years later, the railroad established its division headquarters at Ennis, with several hundred workers at its roundhouse and shops.

EOLA

Central Texas • Concho County • 218

Eola, the name this town adopted in 1901, has been traced to Aeolus, the god of the winds in ancient Greek and Roman mythology.

ERA

Oklahoma border • Cooke County • 200

When early residents of this settlement filled out an application for a post office, they decided to name it after A. H. Hargrove's little daughter, Era. The application was approved in 1878, the child's father became postmaster, and the post office opened at the family's farm home.

ETOILE

East Texas • Nacogdoches County • 70 • ee-TOIL

Residents of Macedonia, a small community 19 miles east of Lufkin, gained a post office in 1886, and selected Etoile, French for "star," as the new name for their village.

EULESS

North central Texas • Tarrant County • 42,900

Originally part of the Peters Colony, this community was named for Adam Euless, who came here with his wife from Tennessee and built a home and cotton gin. Euless was a small town until the mid-1950s, when its transformation into a busy Metroplex suburb began.

EVADALE

Southeast Texas • Jasper County • 1,753

John H. Kirby, head of the giant Kirby Lumber Company, named this town in 1904 to honor Miss Eva Dale, music teacher at the Southeast Texas Male and Female College in Jasper.

EVERMAN

North central Texas • Tarrant County • 5,700

This town, named for railroad engineer John W. Everman, developed in 1904 when the International & Great Northern Railroad began rail service here. Population soared in the mid-1970s after the new Dallas-Fort Worth International Airport was built nearby.

FABENS
Far west Texas • El Paso County • 5,996 • FAY-b'nz

After the Galveston, Harrisburg & San Antonio rail line reached this area in 1900, a town developed here, named for railroad official George Fabens. Bill Shoemaker, America's greatest horse-racing jockey, was born in Fabens in 1931.

FAIRFIELD
East central Texas • Freestone County • 3,317

Settlers arriving in the 1840s called this place Mount Pleasant, but it was renamed Fairfield in 1851, after being selected as the Freestone County seat. Citizens who had previously lived in Fairfield, Alabama, recommended the new name.

FAIRY
Central Texas • Hamilton County • 31

First called Martin's Gap for frontiersman Jim Martin, this village changed its name when a post office opened here in 1884. The new name honored young Fairy Fort, the daughter of Captain Battle Fort, a local lawyer and Civil War veteran.

FALFURRIAS
South Texas • Brooks County • 5,839 • fal-FOO-rih-uhs

 This town, founded in 1883, was known as La Mota until 1898 when a post office opened with the name Falfurrias. It was likely named for a plant with pale lavender or white flowers that grows wild on the sandy plains here and is also known as sand-verbena, heart's delight, or Lasater's pride.

FANNIN
South Texas • Goliad County • 359

First settlers arriving here established their homes along Perdido Creek, and called their community Perdido, the Spanish word for "lost." In 1889, the Gulf, Western Texas & Pacific rail line was constructed a short distance away, so Perdido's townspeople moved to the railroad.

After the move, the name was changed to Fannin, for Colonel James W. Fannin of the Texas revolutionary army, who was slain along with his troops at Goliad in 1836.

FARMERSVILLE
North central Texas • Collin County • 3,527

The people who built their homes here around 1850 decided to name the community for their main vocation. A town post office opened in 1857, and Farmersville soon became a thriving agricultural and commercial center.

FARWELL
Panhandle • Parmer County • 1,496 • FAHR-w'l

Brothers John V. Farwell and Charles B. Farwell were two of the directors and leading investors in the Capitol Syndicate. After fire destroyed the Texas capitol in 1881, the Chicago-based syndicate agreed to construct a new capitol at Austin—a massive granite building, second in size only to the national capitol in Washington, D.C.—in exchange for 3,050,000 acres in the Texas Panhandle. That land became the vast XIT Ranch, managed by John Farwell. The town of Farwell began in 1905 as an administrative base for the XIT Ranch. In 1907 it was chosen to replace Parmerton as county seat.

FATE
Northeast Texas • Rockwall County • 440

Originating in 1888 as a station on the Missouri-Kansas-Texas Railroad, this town attracted residents from the nearby community of Fate, who relocated along with their businesses, post office, and town name. The name Fate had nothing to do with the force that predetermines events, representing instead the nickname of either Lafayette Brown, a lawman, or Lafayette Peyton, owner of a cotton gin. Which one is a matter of dispute.

FLAT
Central Texas • Coryell County • 210

The small settlement here was known first as Mesquite Flat because of its level terrain and abundant mesquite trees. When residents sought to obtain a post office, postal officials thought the name would be confused with the Mesquite post office in Dallas County, so in 1897 the name was shortened to Flat.

FLATONIA
Central Texas • Fayette County • 1,427

This town was established in 1874 on the Galveston, Harrisburg & San Antonio Railroad right-of-way and named for F. W. Flato, a pioneer merchant.

FLOMOT
Northwest Texas • Motley County • 181 • FLOH-maht

Because of its original location on the line between Floyd and Motley counties, this town's post office took a name in 1902 that combined the first three letters of each county's name.

FLORESVILLE
South Texas • Wilson County • 6,367 • FLOH-res-vil

Floresville was named to honor the Flores family, prominent ranchers in the area. Josefa Augustina Flores de Abrego Barker, a descendant of the first settler, Don Francisco Flores de Abrego, donated 200 acres to be developed as a townsite a few years before the San Antonio & Aransas Pass rail line reached the area in the 1880s.

FLOWER MOUND
North central Texas • Denton County • 42,500

Flower Mound began as a small settlement near a Presbyterian church and cemetery around 1855. It was named for a hill covered with wild-flowers. The town's rapid suburban growth started in the 1970s and has continued since.

FLOYDADA
Northwest Texas • Floyd County • 3,912 • floi-DAY-duh

This Floyd County community was originally called Floyd City. Both the county and town names commemorate Dolphin Ward Floyd, who died in the Battle of the Alamo. In the year 1890, James Price donated 640 acres of land for a townsite, and a post office opened with the name Floydada, combining Floyd with the name of Price's mother, Ada.

Forney

Northeast Texas • Kaufman County • 5,000

Colonel John W. Forney, editor of the *Philadelphia Press* and a director of the Texas & Pacific Railway, met with Dallas officials in 1872 about plans to provide Dallas an east-west rail route. The tracks were completed in 1873. Residents voted to name this town on the rail line in honor of Colonel Forney, who in his newspaper described Texas hospitality and the success of the negotiations.

Forsan

West Texas • Howard County • 291 • FOHR-san

Oil drillers found four different pay sands in 1926 on Clayton Stewart's ranch and, from "four sands," the name Forsan was coined. Stewart donated the land on which this town developed, and its post office opened in 1929.

Fort Davis

Far west Texas • Jeff Davis County • 1,212

Jeff Davis County took its name in 1887 for Jefferson Davis, president of the Confederacy. This town and the military post established here in 1854 were also named for Davis, but in the decade before the Civil War, while he served in the cabinet of President Franklin Pierce. Fort Davis originated as a rough frontier settlement adjacent to the army post. Its population fell after the fort was abandoned in the late 1880s, but later rebounded.

Fort Stockton

Far west Texas • Pecos County • 9,304

The U.S. Army fort established here in 1859 was named for Robert Field Stockton, the young naval officer who, in 1845, delivered to the Texas government the decree granting statehood. Stockton later served with distinction in the Navy during the Mexican War and represented New Jersey in the U.S. Senate. Land developer Peter Gallagher established a town here in 1868 that he named St. Gall. Citizens renamed it Fort Stockton in 1881, five years before the fort was closed.

The Fort Worth stockyards. Courtesy of Ray Miller.

FORT WORTH

North central Texas • Tarrant County • 490,500

The military post established here in 1849 to provide protection from Indian raids was named for General William Jenkins Worth, a hero of the Mexican War. As the civilian community flourished, the town was selected as county seat in 1860. After the Civil War, it became a major shipping and supply depot for cattlemen. The Texas & Pacific Railway arrived to great fanfare in 1876, and one of the welcoming speakers predicted enthusiastically that Fort Worth would eventually reach a population of 5,000. A second railroad arrived in 1880, stockyards were established, and the town became a major beef processing center.

FRANCITAS

Gulf Coast • Jackson County • 143 • fran-SEE-tuhs

A small number of French families settled here in the late 1890s. Employees of the St. Louis, Brownsville & Mexico Railroad began referring to the community as Francitas, Spanish for "Little France."

FREDERICKSBURG

Central Texas • Gillespie County • 8,613

German colonists who arrived by wagon train from New Braunfels founded Fredericksburg in 1846. They named their settlement for King Frederick the Great of Prussia. In 1848 Fredericksburg became the seat of Gillespie County. It remains proud of native son Admiral Chester Nimitz, commander of the U.S. Pacific Fleet in World War II.

FREEPORT

Gulf Coast • Brazoria County • 13,638

Founders of the Freeport Sulphur Company, which developed sulphur deposits in the area, established this town in 1912 and named it for the company. In 1929 the Brazos River was diverted into a new channel, its old channel became a tidal estuary to accommodate large vessels, and the town's harbor became a base for the Gulf of Mexico's largest fleet of commercial shrimp trawlers.

FREER

South Texas • Duval County • 3,299

Daniel J. Freer owned the farm home where this town's first post office opened in 1925. His daughter-in-law, Minnie, was postmaster. After oil was discovered in 1928, Minnie's husband, Charles, bought and developed the townsite, which grew rapidly. The adjacent Piedras Pintas field was described in 1933 as the nation's second largest oil field. While Freer was a boom town for only a few years, it remains a petrochemical center.

FRESNO
Southeast Texas • Fort Bend County • 4,412

An early settler said this area's climate and terrain reminded him of his former home in Fresno, California. The town's population numbered 125 or less through the 1950s but then climbed as metropolitan growth spread from Houston.

FRIENDSWOOD
Southeast Texas • Galveston and Harris counties • 29,938

Friendswood derived its name from a colony of the Society of Friends, or Quakers, established in this wooded area in 1895. It remained a small village until the 1960s, when the NASA Manned Spacecraft Center was built ten miles away and Friendswood became a residential suburb.

FRIONA
Panhandle • Parmer County • 3,909 • free-OH-nuh

This town near the Frio Draw—Frio is the Spanish word for "cold"—became a cattle-shipping point on the Pecos & Northern Texas Railroad in 1898. In 1907, when a post office was established, the town name gained an extra syllable. Friona developed on tracts of land subdivided from the giant XIT Ranch and sold by real estate agent George Wright on behalf of the Capitol Syndicate.

FRISCO
North central Texas • Collin County • 23,050

This community, established around 1900, was first named Emerson for Frank Emerson, a banker in nearby McKinney. A post office opened here in 1904 with the new name Frisco, for the St. Louis, San Francisco & Texas Railway, "the Frisco system," which extended its tracks through the area.

FULTON
Gulf Coast • Aransas County • 864

Fulton, located on Aransas Bay, was named for George Ware Fulton, cousin of steamship inventor Robert Fulton and native of Philadelphia. George Fulton served in the Texas revolutionary army, married the daughter of former governor Henry Smith, worked for the *Baltimore Sun* and various railroads in the North for two decades, then returned to Texas and engaged in ranching and cattle-raising. The village of Fulton is located on the bay where the Fultons built a three-story mansion, completed in 1873. George Fulton developed this town, which by the mid-1880s had a post office, beef-canning factory, school, several churches, and daily stage transport to other towns. The town's name changed to Aransas City around 1890 but then changed back to Fulton ten years later.

GAIL
West Texas • Borden County • 189

This small county seat was named in 1891 for Gail Borden, Jr. Borden, a native of Norwich, New York, succeeded his brother in 1830 as surveyor for Stephen F. Austin's Texas colony. He later patented a process for condensing milk in a vacuum and founded the Borden Milk Company.

GAINESVILLE
Oklahoma border • Cooke County • 15,185

Gainesville, founded in 1850 as the Cooke County seat, took its name for Edmund P. Gaines, a U.S. Army general who aided the cause of Texas independence. The town's first courthouse, a log building, was demolished by a steer trying to shake off pesky flies.

GALENA PARK
Southeast Texas • Harris County • 11,068

Galena Park was named in 1935 for the Galena Signal Oil Company, builder of this town's first oil refinery. For the previous hundred years, the town had been known as Clinton. The name change coincided with development of Houston as a major port and Galena Park's growth as an industrial suburb of Houston.

GALVESTON
Gulf Coast • Galveston County • 65,104

In the eighteenth century, explorer Jose de Hevia named Galveston Bay and Galveston Island in honor of Bernardo de Galvez, Spain's viceroy to Mexico. The notorious pirate Jean Lafitte settled here in 1817 and, while occupying the island, did much entertaining aboard his ship

A scene along the Galveston seawall, built after the 1900 storm. Courtesy of the Rosenberg Library, Galveston, Texas.

and at his fortress home, the Maison Rouge. The U.S. government expelled him in 1821, and other settlers, many from the West Indies, began to arrive. In 1825, Mexico declared the island a port of entry and a customs house opened. Galveston briefly served as capital of the Republic of Texas, but the republic later sold part of the island to developer Michel Menard. Galveston was incorporated in 1839 and grew rapidly. For years it reigned as the state's largest and richest—and most fashionable—city. Disaster came in 1900, with a hurricane that claimed 5,000 to 7,000 lives.

GANADO

Gulf Coast • Jackson County • 1,953 • guh-NAY-doh

Ganado is a Spanish word meaning "cattle" or "herd of livestock." When the Galveston, Harrisburg & San Antonio Railroad laid its tracks through this area in 1881 and 1882, it established a station here, named Ganado by a railroad official who observed a herd of cattle from the train window.

GARCIASVILLE

Far south Texas • Starr County • 1,423

Garciasville was named for Ygnacio Garcia, an early settler who donated the land for the community's Ygnacio de Loyola mission church about 1886. The town developed as a supply center for area ranches and a market for vegetable growers.

GARDEN CITY
West Texas • Glasscock County • 293

When Glasscock County was organized in 1893, Garden City became the county seat. This community developed around a small store operated by William Gardner, agent for an Ohio land company, who, at the urging of his store's customers, submitted the name "Gardner City" on an application for a town post office. Apparently because of poor penmanship on the application or some other error, postal officials in Washington granted approval for a post office named Garden City.

GARLAND
North central Texas • Dallas County • 200,050

District Judge Tom Nash ended the bitter rivalry between two villages, Embree and Duck Creek, by persuading President Grover Cleveland's administration to relocate the Embree post office halfway between the two communities and rename it. The new post office was named in honor of A. H. Garland, Cleveland's attorney general, and Embree and Duck Creek merged into the single town of Garland in the 1880s.

GARY
Louisiana border • Panola County • 280

In the 1880s, when the Gulf, Colorado & Santa Fe extended its rail line southward from Carthage, railroad officials named this place Zuber. In 1900, Smith Garrison and Thomas Hull established a town here, and Garrison had its post office named for his grandson, Gary Sanford. In the town's early days, a sawmill and the Red Dog Saloon were leading enterprises. Outdoor wrestling matches were held each Saturday.

GATESVILLE
Central Texas • Coryell County • 12,415

In 1854 voters chose land owned by Richard Grant as the site of the Coryell County seat. Grant planned the townsite and sold residential and business lots in a public auction. The town took its name from nearby Fort Gates, one in a line of forts built during the Indian wars.

GEORGETOWN
Central Texas • Williamson County • 22,582

Founded in 1848 as the county seat, Georgetown was named for George Washington Glasscock, Sr., who contributed land for the townsite. The establishment of Southwestern University in 1873 and construction of the Georgetown Railroad line bolstered the town's agricultural economy.

GEORGE WEST
South Texas • Live Oak County • 2,834

This town was named for its founder, George Washington West, who in 1912 donated $100,000 and 13 miles of right-of-way through his ranch to the San Antonio, Uvalde & Gulf Railroad to induce it to route its tracks through this county. When the railroad officials agreed, West selected a townsite, installed utilities, and built a school and a hotel. He also paid for construction of two steel bridges across the Nueces River.

GERONIMO
South central Texas • Guadalupe County • 400

German settlers moved to this area in the early 1860s, and the community gradually grew enough for a post office to be established in 1889. The town and post office took their names for Geronimo Creek, which flows through Guadalupe County, but the name has no relation to the famed Apache chieftain. Instead, the creek was named for the San Geronimo Ranch, owned by Jose Antonio Navarro, a leader of the Texas republic. The ranch was established around 1824, several years before Chief Geronimo was born.

GIDDINGS
Central Texas • Lee County • 4,602

Giddings got its start in 1871 when the Houston & Texas Central built its railroad tracks through Lee County and a post office opened here. Local historians generally agree that the town was named for Jabez Demming Giddings, a lawyer, banker, and member of the railroad's board of directors. However, it is possible that the town was instead named for his brother, Congressman DeWitt Clinton Giddings.

GILMER

Northeast Texas • Upshur County • 5,377

Secretary of the Navy Thomas W. Gilmer was killed along with Secretary of State Abel Upshur in an 1844 shipboard explosion. This town, named for Gilmer, became county seat in 1846 and gained a post office in 1856. The importance of sweet potatoes, grown here since the 1890s, to the local economy led to an annual community festival called the East Texas Yamboree.

GLADEWATER

Northeast Texas • Gregg and Upshur counties • 6,329

The Texas & Pacific Railway, building through this area in 1872, founded Gladewater in northwest Gregg County near the Upshur County line. Inhabitants of St. Clair and Point Pleasant moved to Gladewater after their communities were bypassed by the railroad. Gladewater, named for nearby Glade Creek, grew slowly for more than four decades but became an oil boom town for several years in the 1930s.

GLEN ROSE

Central Texas • Somervell County • 2,250

In 1849, George Bernard established a trading post here called Bernard's Mills, bought in 1870 by Thomas C. Jordan. Jordan renamed it Glen Rose at the suggestion of his wife. Mrs. Jordan said the name came to her mind as she viewed wild roses growing in a small valley. Glen Rose, the Somervell County seat, later erected a statue of a dinosaur at the county courthouse. It is the unofficial "dinosaur capital" of the nation, because dinosaur tracks are visible on the limestone bed of the Paluxy River within Dinosaur Valley State Park.

GOLIAD

South Texas • Goliad County • 2,256

First inhabited by Aramana Indians, in 1749 this area became the location of a Spanish fortress and mission, both known popularly as La Bahia. Officials of the Mexican state of Coahuila-Texas declared the fortress a town in 1829. They called it Goliad, an anagram of (H)idalgo, the name of a patriot of the Mexican independence movement. Later, "Remember Goliad!" became a battle cry of the Texas Revolution after Colonel James Fannin and his men were massacred here.

Mission La Bahia in Goliad. Courtesy of Ray Miller.

GONZALES
South central Texas • Gonzales County • 6,459

Named for Rafael Gonzales, governor of the Mexican state of Coahuila-Texas, this community was settled in 1825 as the capital of Green DeWitt's Texas colony. Major James Kerr drew up plans for the town and selected its name. The first skirmish of the Texas Revolution took place here, making this town "the Lexington of Texas."

GRAFORD
North central Texas • Palo Pinto County • 622 • GRAY-ferd

This community first developed in the 1880s. Its post office opened in 1894 with the name Graford, for the town's location midway between Graham and Weatherford. Oil and gas production and recreation at nearby Possum Kingdom Lake have benefited Graford's economy.

GRAHAM

North central Texas • Young County • 8,822 • GRAY-'m

In 1872 two brothers from Kentucky, Edwin and Gus Graham, bought 125,000 acres of land here from the Peters Colony at 17 cents an acre. They established the town of Graham and the Graham Brothers Salt Works.

GRANBURY

Central Texas • Hood County • 5,523

Hiram Bronson Granbury, a Confederate Army brigadier general who led a unit of Texans, died in combat and is buried here in the town named for him.

GRAND PRAIRIE

North central Texas • Dallas County • 111,400

When the Texas & Pacific Railway extended its tracks westward from Dallas to the prairie village of Deckman, around 1875, railroad officials decided to change the town name to reflect the local terrain.

GRAND SALINE

Northeast Texas • Van Zandt County • 2,946 • gran suh-LEEN

A vast salt dome underlies Grand Saline. John Jordan, first settler in this area, began a primitive salt works in 1845. The settlement that sprang up around the salt works was called Jordan's Saline until 1873, when the Texas & Pacific Railway arrived and built a depot named Grand Saline. Morton Salt Company later became the sole owner of the salt operations, with hundreds of local employees.

GRAPEVINE

North central Texas • Tarrant, Dallas, and Denton counties • 36,450

Settlers began to arrive in this area during the 1840s, and a post office opened here in 1858. It was given the name Grape Vine because of wild grapes growing in the area. The name was later condensed to a single word. Through the first two thirds of the twentieth century, Grapevine remained relatively untouched by urban growth, but this rapidly changed with the construction of Dallas-Fort Worth International Airport at the southeastern edge of the town.

Greenville C of C Foundation Station
Honoring Hunt County Native
Major Audie L. Murphy
May 23, 1998
Greenville, TX 75401

GREENVILLE
Northeast Texas • Hunt County • 24,362

This county seat was named for Thomas Green, a Virginia native, who joined the Texas revolutionary army and fought in the Battle of San Jacinto. Later, he became a Confederate Army brigadier general and was killed during an 1864 battle at Blair's Landing on the Red River. Audie Murphy, America's most decorated soldier in World War II, was born in the Kingston community north of Greenville.

GROESBECK
East central Texas • Limestone County • 3,663 • GROHZ-bek

In 1870 the Houston & Texas Central Railway extended its tracks to the center of Limestone County and founded this town. It was named for one of the railroad's directors, Abram Groesbeeck, but when postal officials in Washington processed the application for a town post office, they omitted one "e."

GROVES
Southeast Texas • Jefferson County • 16,692

This community became known as Pecan Groves after a Port Arthur nursery company, Griffing Brothers, planted 6,000 pecan trees on a 385-acre tract here in 1910. The first word of the name was later dropped. With its location near the intercoastal waterway and on the Kansas City Southern Railway line, Groves became one of the coastal area's industrial centers in the late 1930s.

Gun Barrel City
East Texas • Henderson County • 4,233

Gun Barrel City began developing in the 1960s on the eastern shore of the Cedar Creek Reservoir. Residents voted to incorporate in 1974—a move that enabled local establishments to sell beer and wine. The town name comes from a community symbol, a rifle, and the motto "We Shoot Straight With You."

Gunsight
North central Texas • Stephens County • 6

A settlement developed around J. W. Shepherd's general store in 1879, and during the following year a post office opened at the store. It was named for nearby Gunsight Mountain. The mountain rises about 200 feet over the surrounding terrain, and its shape reminded early settlers of a gunsight atop the barrel of a gun.

Guy
Southeast Texas • Fort Bend County • 60

As farm families moved into this area, a post office opened in 1898. It was named for a young polio victim, Unaguy Rowland, daughter of early settlers.

Hale Center
Northwest Texas • Hale County • 2,098

This town came into being in 1893 when Epworth and Hale City, two rival villages founded in 1891, merged and adopted the name Hale Center. The new town was in the center of Hale County, which had been named for a hero of the Texas Revolution, John C. Hale.

Hallettsville
South Texas • Lavaca County • 2,889

A predominantly German-Czech community founded in 1838, Hallettsville is located halfway between San Antonio and Houston. It was named for Mrs. John Hallett, donor of land for the townsite, and was designated the Lavaca County seat in 1852. Robert Ripley's syndicated "Believe It or Not" feature once pointed out to readers that, in 1913, Hallettsville, a town with 13 letters in its name, had a population of 1,300 and "13 churches, 13 newspapers, and 13 saloons."

HAMILTON
Central Texas • Hamilton County • 2,999

This county seat, like its county, was named in 1858 for James Hamilton, governor of South Carolina in the early 1830s and a supporter of the Texas cause of independence. Hamilton volunteered to help the Republic of Texas obtain much-needed loans and to represent President Mirabeau Lamar in treaty negotiations with European powers.

HAPPY
Panhandle • Swisher and Randall counties • 652

Happy's name came from Happy Draw, a creek bed two miles away where, in the last century, thirsty cowboys often found running water. Hugh Currie, the town's first settler, built a home in 1891 that also came to be Happy's post office and the location of the area's first telephone. In 1908, the First State Bank of Happy was chartered.

HARLINGEN
Far south Texas • Cameron County • 57,240 • HAHR-lin-juhn

Founder Lon Hill named this town in 1904 as a tribute to railroad promoter Uriah Lott. Lott was a descendant of the Van Harlingen family, whose ancestral home was the Dutch coastal town of Harlingen.

HASKELL
Northwest Texas • Haskell County • 3,124

Once an Indian campsite, this location attracted settlers in the early 1880s and was called Rice Springs after Rice Durrett, an employee of the Reynolds & Matthews Cattle Company. A general store opened, as did the Road to Ruin saloon, where church services were held on Sundays. The town became the Haskell County seat and renamed itself Haskell in 1885. The name honored Charles R. Haskell, a teenager from Tennessee who quit school and joined a group of Tennessee volunteers who fought in the Texas Revolution. Haskell was slain in the Goliad massacre.

HAWKINS

Northeast Texas • Wood County • 1,439

A village sprang up here in 1873 when the Texas & Pacific Railway extended its tracks through Wood County. It was reportedly named for a member of the railroad's surveying crew who left his name, Hawkins, carved on a tree.

HEARNE

East central Texas • Robertson County • 5,150

Houston & Texas Central Railway officials named this town for Christopher Columbus Hearne and his family, pioneer landowners in Robertson County. When he heard a rumor in 1855 about their planned railroad, Christopher Hearne traveled to Houston and offered H&TC promoters a right-of-way and a townsite to develop if they would establish a rail shipping station in this area on the Brazos River. They accepted the offer and told him the townsite would be named Hearne. The project was delayed by the Civil War, but afterward Hearne's widow deeded 700 acres to the railroad company, and trains arrived at a Hearne depot in 1868. A post office opened in 1869, and the town soon had general stores, saloons, cotton gins, a Masonic hall, a drugstore, churches, two hotels, and a newspaper, the *Hearne Enterprise.*

HEBBRONVILLE

South Texas • Jim Hogg County • 4,346 • HEB-r'n-vil

Hebbronville, the Jim Hogg County seat, was named for rancher James R. Hebbron, who arranged for a townsite at this location when the Texas Mexican Railway constructed its rail line through the area. By the time a post office opened in 1895, the town consisted of about 150 inhabitants, with a general store and a school taught by Rosendo Berrara. Iglesia Catolica Mexicana, the town's first church, was organized in 1899, followed a few years later by Baptist and Methodist congregations.

HEDLEY

Panhandle • Donley County • 440

In the early 1900s Nat Smith was developing a townsite called Rowe near this location on the Fort Worth & Denver City Railway. By 1906, the townsite included a bank, a gin, several stores, a school, and a church.

When a row developed in Rowe between the property owners and Smith, over building restrictions and other matters, the townspeople decided to relocate to a site a mile down the tracks. Businesses joined the move in 1907. Horses and mules hauled the stores and houses to the new townsite. When a post office opened there, it was named for J. E. M. Hedley. Hedley had persuaded the railroad to relocate its depot and loading pens to the new site. Rowe disappeared, while Hedley grew as a commercial center for the surrounding farm and ranch area.

HELOTES
South Texas • Bexar County • 1,958 • hel-OH-tis

Mexican settlers came to this vicinity in the 1850s and founded a community called Helotes. Various explanations have been given for the town's name, Spanish for "green ear of corn." One historian avers that the first settler, a man named Chaca, named the place after building a hut and planting a cornfield. Another attributes the name to early settlers who discovered that the corn they grew was often taken by Indians when in the roasting-ear stage.

HEMPSTEAD
Southeast Texas • Waller County • 4,058

Hempstead was named for Dr. G. B. S. Hempstead, a brother-in-law and benefactor of Dr. Richard Peebles. Peebles and James W. McDade established this town in 1856 at the proposed terminus of the Houston & Texas Central Railway. When the first train arrived in mid-1858, the occasion drew a crowd estimated at 3,000.

HENDERSON
East Texas • Rusk County • 11,951

Henderson was founded and chosen as the Rusk County seat in 1843. William B. Ochiltree donated land for the townsite with the proviso that it be named for his friend J. Pinckney Henderson, a San Augustine lawyer who later became the first governor of Texas and then a U.S. senator.

HENRIETTA
Oklahoma border • Clay County • 3,040

In 1857, the Texas Legislature organized Clay County, named it for statesman Henry Clay, and designated that the county seat be named

Henrietta. There are several theories as to why the feminine form of Henry was chosen. One local historian avers that it combines the first names of two early settlers, Henry and Etta Parish. Another observes that one of Henry Clay's six daughters was named Henrietta.

HEREFORD
Panhandle • Deaf Smith County • 14,910 • HER-ferd

When residents filed an application for a post office in the late 1890s, postal authorities rejected the proposed name, Blue Water, and asked for another. The applicants next submitted Hereford, the name of a breed of cattle raised on area ranches.

HEWITT
Central Texas • McLennan County • 10,538 • HYOO-it

Hewitt was established in 1882 when the Missouri-Kansas-Texas Railroad crossed McLennan County and built a station at this location eight miles south of Waco. The community was named for George A. Hewitt, a railroad official. New residents commuting to work in Waco have boosted Hewitt's population in recent decades.

HIDALGO
Far south Texas • Hidalgo County • 5,084 • hih-DAL-goh

Members of Jose de Escandon's colony inhabited this area as early as 1774. It was later the site of a trading post established in 1851 by John Young and two partners. While Young had called it Edinburgh for his native city in Scotland, in 1885 postal officials gave the town the same name as the county, Hidalgo, after Mexican patriot Miguel Hidalgo y Costilla.

HIGH ISLAND
Gulf Coast • Galveston County • 500

With an elevation of 47 feet, this town is the highest point between Sabine Pass and Point Bolivar. It has often been a place of refuge for Bolivar Peninsula residents to escape floodwaters during Gulf of Mexico storms.

HIGHLANDS
Southeast Texas • Harris County • 8,140

Early in the twentieth century, Highlands originated as Elena, a rural community between Houston and Baytown. The name Highlands was adopted in 1929 and refers to the site where the town was founded, on the east bank of the San Jacinto River, which is higher than the west bank.

HILLISTER
Southeast Texas • Tyler County • 200

Hillister's name originated through a clerical error. Local historians agree that when an application for a post office was sent to Washington in 1882, the proposed name was either misspelled or misread, but they don't know for certain what that name was. One historian believes the proposed post office name was Hollister, for railroad builder W. H. Hollister. Another believes that it was Hallister, for two brothers who operated a local sawmill.

HILLSBORO
Central Texas • Hill County • 7,757

Hillsboro and Hill County are named for Dr. George W. Hill, a surgeon from Tennessee, who served as secretary of war in President Sam Houston's cabinet and was later elected to the Texas Legislature from Navarro County. The town name was first spelled Hillsborough but was shortened by postal officials in 1888.

HITCHCOCK
Gulf Coast • Galveston County • 6,560

This town was called Highland by the settlers who began to build their homes here on the Highland Bayou in the 1840s. The Gulf, Colorado & Santa Fe Railway extended its tracks here in the 1870s, and in 1873 the railroad named the town Hitchcock in honor of Lent M. Hitchcock, a naval officer and Galveston civic leader.

HOLLIDAY
North central Texas • Archer County • 1,586

Holliday was named for Captain John J. Holliday, a member of the Texas revolutionary army who was one of the few survivors of the Goliad massacre. While a member of the Texan Santa Fe Expedition in 1841, Holliday carved his name on a tree at the mouth of a little creek, unknowingly giving his name to the town later founded here.

HONDO
Southwest Texas • Medina County • 6,960 • HAHN-doh

Hondo took its name from nearby Hondo Creek. In Spanish the name means "deep." Sale of town lots began in 1881 after the first train arrived here on the Galveston, Harrisburg & San Antonio Railway line. Medina County voters approved Hondo as their new county seat, replacing Castroville, in 1892.

HONEY GROVE
Oklahoma border • Fannin County • 1,832

According to local lore, legendary frontiersman David Crockett, en route from Tennessee to join the Texas revolutionary army, spent several days hunting in this area, found one of the trees filled with wild honey, and called his campsite "Honey Grove."

HOUSTON
Southeast Texas • Harris County • 1,818,613

Houston was named for General Sam Houston, commander of Texas forces during the Texas Revolution and two-term president of the Republic of Texas. After the republic became a state, he served nearly 14 years in the U. S. Senate. In 1836, brothers Augustus and John K. Allen decided to develop a new town, which they named Houston, to replace the town of Harrisburg burned by Santa Anna's troops before the Battle of San Jacinto. The town platted by the Allen brothers—destined to become the fourth largest city in the United States—served as capital of the fledgling Republic of Texas for three years. Buffalo Bayou, flowing from Houston into Galveston Bay, provided access for barges and small steamboats and helped turn Houston into a major trade center long

Sam Houston. Courtesy of Mrs. F. T. Baldwin Collection, Sam Houston Regional Library.

before its ship channel was constructed. Railroads were crucial to the city's growth; in the mid-nineteenth century, Houston promoted itself as the place "Where Eleven Railroads Meet the Sea." Completion of the ship channel, a deepwater harbor, and a turning basin made Houston an official ocean port, and by 1930 forty oil companies had offices in Houston.

HUBBARD

Central Texas • Hill County • 1,667

This community, settled around 1860 and known as Slap-Out and McLainsboro, became Hubbard after the St. Louis Southwestern Railway established a station here in 1881. A meeting of citizens decided to name the town in honor of Richard B. Hubbard, Jr., governor of Texas from 1876 to 1879 and later U.S. minister to Japan.

HUMBLE

Southeast Texas • Harris County • 14,956

After oil strikes in 1904 and 1905, this village of 700, named for pioneer settler Pleasant Smith Humble, found itself in the middle of the largest producing field in Texas. The oil boom boosted the town's population to 10,000 within a decade. Humble Oil & Refining Company, the predecessor to Exxon USA, was incorporated in 1911 by a group of the oil field's operators. One of them, Ross Sterling, later became governor of Texas.

HUNTSVILLE

Southeast Texas • Walker County • 34,393

Pleasant and Ephraim Gray founded this town as an Indian trading post in the mid-1830s and named it for the Gray family's former home town, Huntsville, Alabama. After Texas achieved statehood, Huntsville lost in its bid to be the state capital but was chosen in 1847 as the location of the state penitentiary. Another type of state institution was established in 1879: Sam Houston Normal Institute, later Sam Houston State University.

HURST
North central Texas • Tarrant County • 36,250

This community was named for early settler W. L. "Billy" Hurst, who moved his family from Tennessee to Texas in 1870. He donated land in 1903 to the Rock Island Railroad so that tracks could be laid through this area and a depot constructed. Trains seldom stopped, however, because of Hurst's tiny size—it had only one or two dozen residents—until the 1940s, when it became a bedroom community for Fort Worth and Dallas.

HYE
Central Texas • Blanco County • 105

This hamlet was named for Hiram "Hye" Brown, who established its first general store in 1880. The town's first post office opened in the store in 1886, with Brown as postmaster. Because young Lyndon Johnson mailed his first letter here when he was four years old, a special event took place at the Hye post office on November 3, 1965: the swearing-in ceremony of Postmaster General Lawrence O'Brien, appointed by President Johnson.

IDALOU
Northwest Texas • Lubbock County • 2,107

Idalou originated in 1915 as a settlement on the South Plains & Santa Fe rail line, 12 miles northeast of Lubbock. The town was named for Ida and Louise Bassett, sisters of rancher and land promoter Julian M. Bassett.

IMPERIAL
Southwest Texas • Pecos County • 360

Settlers who came to this Pecos River valley in the early 1900s believed it might become the equal of California's famed Imperial Valley and named their town accordingly. But prospective land buyers soon found that high saline levels in the valley's irrigated water made farming unproductive.

Industry

Southeast Texas • Austin County • 475

Friedrich Ernst, an immigrant from Germany, arrived here with his family in 1831 and sought to induce more Germans to come to Texas. As a market for tobacco grew, Ernst established a cigar-making industry with diligent German workers, who inspired the name given to this town.

Inez

Gulf Coast • Victoria County • 1,515

The original community at this location was known as Arenosa. In 1882, the New York, Texas & Mexican Railway built a station here on its new rail line. It named the adjacent townsite Inez in honor of Inez Hungerford. She was the wife of Daniel E. Hungerford and a daughter of Count Joseph Telfener, partners in organizing the railroad and securing its charter. The same year, the town of Hungerford in Wharton County, also on the New York, Texas & Mexican line, was named for Inez's husband.

Ingleside

Gulf Coast • San Patricio County • 7,570

In the early 1850s, when J. W. Vineyard and other pioneer settlers bought land and built homes here, Vineyard adopted the Gaelic word for "fireside" as this community's name. Coincidentally, prosperous vineyards were established here in the 1880s.

Iola

Southeast Texas • Grimes County • 331

Iola is believed to have taken its name from one of Stephen F. Austin's colonists, Edward Ariola, who settled in this area around 1836. Some argue instead that the name came from a local Indian tribe. At first the community was so small that Zion Methodist Church, built in 1852, also served as a schoolhouse. But when the Trinity & Brazos Valley rail line was built through here in 1907 and an adjacent townsite developed, Iola's population grew to 300.

IOWA PARK
Oklahoma border • Wichita County • 6,996

D. C. Kolp, a native Iowan, established a townsite here in 1888 at a station on the Fort Worth & Denver City rail line, and began advertising the town to residents of his home state. Iowa Park developed into a farm market center. Population rose with the discovery of oil close by in the 1920s and with the establishment in the 1940s of Sheppard Field, an Army Air Corps training base.

IRAAN
Southwest Texas • Pecos County • 1,313 • eye-ruh-ANN

When oil was discovered on Ira G. Yates' ranch in 1926, Yates planned a townsite and offered a lot as first prize in a town name contest. The winning entry, Iraan, combined Yates' given name with that of his wife, Ann. The town of Iraan quickly developed with accommodations for oil field workers and had a population near 3,000 while drilling was most active in the Yates field.

IRVING
North central Texas • Dallas County • 180,050

In 1902 Otis Brown and J. O. Schulze began promoting a townsite located northwest of Dallas on the Chicago, Rock Island & Gulf rail line. At the suggestion of Brown's wife, the townsite was named for author Washington Irving. Like several other towns in Dallas County, Irving grew steadily. In 1970, its new Texas Stadium became the home of the Dallas Cowboys, and in 1990 Exxon moved its corporate headquarters from New York City to Irving.

ITALY
Central Texas • Ellis County • 2,017

Gabriel Penn proposed the name of this community because, he said, the climate reminded him of "sunny Italy." By the 1920s, Italy was a cotton-farming center and home to a cottonseed oil mill, five gins, and a cotton compress.

ITASCA
Central Texas • Hill County • 1,622 • eye-TAS-kuh

Most historians believe that this town, founded in 1881, was named by a former Minnesotan for Lake Itasca in his home state. Texas folklorist J. Frank Dobie, however, dissented. "The name of Itasca is a descendant of *atasca* (Spanish, 'it sticks'), a reference to the black-waxy soil on which the village is situated," said Dobie.

IVANHOE
Oklahoma border • Fannin County • 110

Joe Dupree had just finished reading Sir Walter Scott's novel *Ivanhoe* when postal officials requested a name for the post office to be established here. The Ivanhoe post office opened in 1887.

JACINTO CITY
Southeast Texas • Harris County • 9,844 • juh-sin-toh SIT-ee

Jacinto City was virtually a wartime creation. A residential subdivision that was developed here just before Pearl Harbor Day became home to hundreds of war plant and shipyard workers. Jacinto City, which derived its name from the historic San Jacinto battlefield nearby, incorporated in 1947 and voters elected grocer Inch Chandler as mayor.

JACKSBORO
North central Texas • Jack County • 3,531

Farmers and their families began settling this area about 1854 and called their community Mesquiteville. In 1856, state legislators designated Mesquiteville as the Jack County seat and renamed it in honor of brothers Patrick C. and William H. Jack, who fought for Texas independence from Mexico.

JACKSONVILLE
East Texas • Cherokee County • 13,275

In 1847 Jackson Smith moved to this site on Gum Creek from his native Kentucky and established a blacksmith's shop. Dr. William Jackson, who came from Jacksonville, Illinois, built a home near Smith's shop and arranged for a townsite to be platted. Residents of Gum Creek decided to change the town's name to Jacksonville, drawing on the names of both the physician and the blacksmith.

JASPER
Southeast Texas • Jasper County • 8,004

Both this county seat and its county were named for Sergeant William Jasper, a hero of the American Revolution, who died fighting at Savannah in 1779. In 1865, the weekly *Jasper News-Boy* began publishing—and continues to publish today.

JEFFERSON
Northeast Texas • Marion County • 2,425

The developers who laid out this townsite in the early 1840s on Big Cypress Creek decided to name it for Thomas Jefferson. Jefferson was strategically located for steamship access to the Mississippi River via Big Cypress Bayou, Caddo Lake, and the Red River. It quickly grew into the state's second most important port, shipping bales of cotton and receiving shipments of building materials, farm supplies, and household goods for sale to towns throughout northeast Texas.

JOHNSON CITY
Central Texas • Blanco County • 1,196

Area settlers agreed in the mid-1870s to establish a townsite here on the Pedernales River and apply for a post office. James Polk Johnson, a leader of the group and relative of future president Lyndon B. Johnson, donated lots for school houses and constructed an office building, hotel, and gristmill. Settlers named the town after Johnson and succeeded in their petition to make Johnson City the new Blanco County seat.

JOLLY
Oklahoma border • Clay County • 221

Established in 1890 by the Fort Worth & Denver City line, this town served as a rail shipping point for western Clay County. It derived its cheerful name from one of the area's ranchers and farmers, William H. Jolly.

JOSHUA

Central Texas • Johnson County • 4,371

The Gulf, Colorado & Santa Fe Railway platted a townsite and built a depot here, along its line between Fort Worth and Cleburne, in 1881. Families from Caddo Grove, a community two miles away that had been bypassed by the railroad, led settlement of the new town. Townspeople accepted Dr. D. B. McMillan's suggestion to name the town after the biblical Joshua.

JUNCTION

Southwest Texas • Kimble County • 2,869

In 1876, this town took the name Junction City (the word "city" was later dropped) from its location at the confluence of the North and South Llano rivers. It became the Kimble County seat, and until a court house was constructed, officials conducted county business outdoors or in a blacksmith's shop. In 1877, Texas Rangers headquarters were set up here to combat cattle rustlers and other outlaws.

On the Llano River at Junction. Courtesy of Houston Metropolitan Research Center, Houston Public Library.

JUSTICEBURG .

Northwest Texas • Garza County • 76

Justiceburg was established on the ranch of Jefferson Davis Justice, who settled here in 1899 and sold some land to homesteaders. A post office opened at the home of the Arthur Tuffing family in 1902. Mrs. Tuffing named the post office LeForest, after her two sons, Lee and Forest. In 1910, Justice donated a section of land for development of a townsite and as a right-of-way for the Panhandle & Santa Fe Railway line. The town and its post office were named for the rancher, whose son, Appleton Justice, became postmaster.

KAMAY

Oklahoma border • Wichita County • 642 • KAY-im-ay

First known as Kemp City, this town was founded in 1912 by land investors Joe Kemp, W. Munger, and Reese Allen. They sold some acreage to farmers and later organized the K-M-A Oil Company, whose name came from the initial letters of their last names. Postal officials rejected K-M-A as a name for the post office and chose Kamay instead. Citizens nonetheless pronounce their town's name like the three initials and not like Camay soap.

Caddo Lake State Park Station

KARNACK

Northeast Texas • Harrison County • 775

Karnack was named for the Egyptian village of Karnack, which was said to have been as close to the ancient city of Thebes on the Nile as this town was to Port Caddo. Once the northeastern port of entry into the Republic of Texas, Port Caddo became a ghost town after steamboats gave way to trains. Karnack, however, survived and even prospered. It is the birthplace of Lady Bird Johnson, wife of the 36th U.S. president, Lyndon B. Johnson.

KARNES CITY
South Texas • Karnes County • 3,029

A Cuero, Texas, land development firm founded this town in 1891. Like its county, Karnes City was named for Henry W. Karnes, who fought in several battles of the Texas Revolution and was a trusted scout for General Sam Houston.

KATY
Southeast Texas • Harris, Fort Bend, and Waller counties • 11,551

Katy was established along the Missouri-Kansas-Texas Railroad, often called "the Katy Line." Although some historians say that this town was named for the railroad, several prominent citizens attested that it was named in the 1890s for Katy Mares, a local saloonkeeper. "Katy's" was a popular place where railroad construction gangs and other laborers gathered after a day's work.

KAUFMAN
Northeast Texas • Kaufman County • 5,750

Originally called Kingsborough, this town adopted its new name in 1851 when it was designated the county seat. David S. Kaufman, for whom the town and county were named, served in the Congress of the Republic of Texas and later became the first Texas representative seated in the U.S. Congress. By 1900, Kaufman was a well-established trade center for area farmers.

KEENE
Central Texas • Johnson County • 4,483

Jeremiah Easterwood and his family, who came here in 1852, were the first settlers in this town, originally known as Elm Grove. Other settlers arrived around the time the Gulf, Colorado & Santa Fe tracks were laid and a general store opened in the early 1890s. Postal officials selected the name Keene for an unrecorded reason when they established the town's post office in 1894. That same year, Seventh Day Adventist church officials acquired an 836-acre tract that later became the home of Southwestern Adventist University.

KELLER
North central Texas • Tarrant County • 22,450

When the Texas & Pacific Railway began extending its tracks westward from Dallas in the early 1880s, druggist H. W. Wood set aside 40 acres of his land to be donated to the public for a townsite he called Athol. Settlers were attracted to the townsite before the rail line reached the area and urged that a railroad stop be established here. John C. Keller, construction foreman on the railroad project, was said to have arranged for the station to be built if, in exchange, the town were named Keller.

KEMAH
Gulf Coast • Galveston County • 1,462 • KEE-muh

Settled on Galveston Bay around 1898, this town was originally called Evergreen. When a post office opened in 1907, the name was changed to Kemah, an Indian word meaning "facing the winds," because of the gulf breeze. Kemah, a farming community, also became a popular location for fishing camps and vacation homes.

KENDALIA
South central Texas • Kendall County • 76

Like its county, this small village was named for George W. Kendall, an adventurous journalist and author who joined the Texan Santa Fe Expedition in 1841 and covered the Mexican War in 1846. His accounts have been called the first battle coverage by a foreign correspondent. He had learned the printing business as a young man in New England and worked for Horace Greeley. After the war, he engaged in newspaper work for a year in Alabama, went to Louisiana where he co-founded the *New Orleans Picayune,* and then helped pioneer sheep-raising in Texas on his Kendall County ranch. Kendalia developed soon after 1900, with a post office, three stores, and a church.

KENEDY
South Texas • Karnes County • 6,473

Settlers who lived here in the early 1880s named their village Kenedy Junction to honor Mifflin Kenedy, a promotor of the San Antonio &

Aransas Pass Railway, which built its tracks through this community and established a depot here.

KENNARD
East Texas • Houston County • 364 • kuh-NAHRD

Kennard was established in 1902 and named for John E. Kennard, an official of the Central Coal & Coke Company of Kansas City, Missouri. The town developed after the Missouri company bought a huge tract of timberland in 1899, built a sawmill, and established a townsite. The sawmill operations grew larger along with the town, which had about 600 inhabitants by 1915. But by 1920, much of the timber had been cleared, and the mill was closed and dismantled. Ultimately, the area was reforested and became part of the Davy Crockett National Forest.

KENNEDALE
North central Texas • Tarrant County • 5,350

Kennedale took its name for Oliver Kennedy, who surveyed and platted this site in 1886 and encouraged the Southern Pacific Railroad to extend its tracks here. Settlers were already making their homes in this area and a post office opened in 1884. Kennedale grew slowly until World War II, when workers in Fort Worth-area military defense plants began to move to subdivisions in the town.

KERMIT
New Mexico border • Winkler County • 6,529

When a post office opened here in 1910, the town was named for Kermit Roosevelt, a son of President Theodore Roosevelt who had visited the area on a hunting trip in 1908. Kermit was Winkler County's only town until an oil strike in 1926 resulted in the growth of nearby Wink. In 1928, the Texas & Pacific Railway built a branch line to Kermit because of the county's booming oil production.

KERRVILLE
Southwest Texas • Kerr County • 21,042

A small settlement founded here in 1848 by Joshua D. Brown was first known as Brownsborough. Later, after Kerr County formed in 1856, the town became Kerrsville, the county seat. Two years later, the name was changed to Kerrville, dropping the "s." Both the county and county seat were named for James Kerr, one of the "Old 300" settlers of Stephen F. Austin's colony, who served in the Congress of the Republic of Texas. This ranching town's first general merchandise store was opened in 1869 by Captain Charles Schreiner, a native of France who became an early Kerrville settler and founder of a family business empire. The San Antonio & Aransas Pass railroad reached Kerrville in 1887, thanks in large measure to Schreiner's influence. By 1900 the Charles Schreiner Company owned 600,000 acres of land. The merchant and banker developed a cooperative market and warehouse system for wool growers and is credited with making Kerrville the world's mohair center.

KILGORE
Northeast Texas • Gregg County • 11,990

When this town was founded in 1872, it was named for Constantine B. Kilgore, a Rusk County attorney. Kilgore later served in the Texas Senate and the U.S. House of Representatives, and in 1895 was appointed by President Grover Cleveland as a federal judge in the Indian Territory. The decline of the cotton industry and the start of the Great Depression were beginning to have an effect on population when discovery of the East Texas Oil Field, in late 1930, put Kilgore near the center of the region's oil boom. Kilgore drew national attention when, at one time during the boom, there were more than 100 producing wells within the city limits.

KILLEEN
Central Texas • Bell County • 82,145

Settled around 1872 at a location on the Gulf, Colorado & Santa Fe Railway, this town was called Palo Alto before being renamed for Frank Killeen, assistant general manager of the railroad. The town developed as a farming trade center and a shipping point for cotton and grain. Killeen was transformed during World War II when it became the home of the Camp Hood army base, now Fort Hood.

KINGSVILLE
Gulf Coast • Kleburg County • 26,987

Kingsville was established on the Fourth of July, 1904, when the first train arrived here on the St. Louis, Brownsville & Mexico Railway. The first house had been completed the day before. The new townsite, located in the heart of the King Ranch, was named for the ranch's founder, Captain Richard King. The railway company soon transferred its headquarters and maintenance shops to Kingsville. A weekly newspaper began publication and a cotton gin, hotel, and other businesses opened as the town began to grow.

KIRBYVILLE
Southeast Texas • Jasper County • 1,978

Founded in 1895, Kirbyville was named for John Henry Kirby, father of the Texas timber industry. His Kirby Lumber Company once controlled more than 300,000 acres of East Texas forests. Kirbyville's population was estimated at 2,900 in 1914 but fell thereafter.

KLONDIKE
Northeast Texas • Delta County • 175

This area's first settlers were members of the R. W. Hunt family who arrived in 1856. When the Texas Midland Railway extended its tracks through Delta County in 1895, a post office was established and named by Joel Jefferson Hunt for Klondike, Alaska, where the gold rush was in progress.

KNICKERBOCKER
West central Texas • Tom Green County • 50

Joseph Tweedy, a native of New York City, and his partners—Lawrence Grinnell, Morgan Grinnell, and J. B. Reynolds—established the Knickerbocker Ranch in this valley west of San Angelo in 1877. They also founded the Tweedy Mercantile Store and, around 1881, the town of Knickerbocker. The New Yorkers were said to have named the ranch and town for Dietrich Knickerbocker, fictional narrator of Washington Irving's mock-serious *Knickerbocker's History of New York.*

KNOX CITY
Northwest Texas • Knox County • 1,433

Early settlers established a townsite here in 1905, knowing that the Kansas City, Mexico & Orient Railway was extending its tracks toward this location. The townsite was first called Orient, for the railroad. It subsequently became Knox City to correspond to the county name, which was chosen in honor of Henry Knox, a brigadier general during the American Revolution and secretary of war in George Washington's first cabinet. Knox City grew as a farm marketplace known for its seedless watermelons.

Kosciusko
South central Texas • Wilson County • 390 • kuh-SHOOS-koh

Silesian settlers who arrived here around 1890 named their community for Tadeusz Kosciusko, the Polish volunteer who brilliantly distinguished himself in the American revolutionary army and became a major general. He later led Poland's tragic 1794 struggle for independence and democratic reform, which was crushed by Prussian and Russian troops.

Kountze
Southeast Texas • Hardin County • 2,491 • koontz

Located in the center of the Big Thicket National Preserve, Kountze is the Hardin County seat. The town was founded by brothers Herman and Augustus Kountze, employees of the Sabine & East Texas Railroad. In 1881, they laid out a townsite at this location on the west side of the railroad.

Kyle
South central Texas • Hays County • 2,749

Kyle was established in 1880, when Captain Ferguson Kyle and Judge David Moore donated 200 acres of land to the International & Great Northern Railroad for a townsite adjacent to its tracks. The town was named for Kyle, whose daughter, Mary Kyle Hartson, served as mayor from 1943 to 1946, while she was a great-grandmother. During her time as mayor, women filled seven of the nine municipal offices. Mrs. Hartson was later quoted by *Life* as saying, "We balanced the budget and cleaned up the town. Then, when everything was under control, I retired."

LADONIA
Oklahoma border • Fannin County • 709 • luh-DOHN-yuh

In the 1840s, settlers began to arrive in this village known as McCowansville, after the local saloonkeeper, Frank McCowan. According to one historian, McCowan admired the voice of LaDonna Millsap, who arrived here on a wagon train from Tennessee and entertained local families with her singing. McCowan proposed renaming the village LaDonna, and the name evolved into Ladonia.

LA FERIA
Far south Texas • Cameron County • 5,541 • luh FER-ih-uh

In Spanish, La Feria means "the fair" or "the market." Mexican ranchers settled this area in the late 1780s and held fiestas here. Anglo-American settlers came after the St. Louis, Brownsville & Mexico railroad arrived in 1911. A year later, the Cameron County Bank occupied the town's first brick building.

LA GRANGE
Central Texas • Fayette County • 4,303

La Grange became the county seat when this county, named for the Marquis de Lafayette, formed in 1838. The town may have been named for the chateau on Lafayette's estate in France. A more widely held view is that early settlers named La Grange for their home town in Tennessee.

LA GRULLA
Far south Texas • Starr County • 1,752 • lah GROO-yuh

The original Mexican settlement at this site took its name from the Spanish word for "crane." These migrating birds abounded at a lake that existed years ago in the vicinity. A post office named Grulla opened early in the twentieth century, but residents still prefer to call their town La Grulla.

LAIRD HILL
East Texas • Rusk County • 405

Families from Georgia, Alabama, and Tennessee settled in this area in the 1870s and named their community for an early landowner, S. S. Laird. Three days after C. M. (Dad) Joiner struck oil on a farm here in late 1930, Laird Hill and the nearby town of Kilgore swarmed with 10,000 people. During the raucous and sometimes violent days of the East Texas oil boom, the town was widely known as "Pistol Hill" because of the frequency of tavern brawls that ended in gunfights.

LAKE JACKSON
Gulf Coast • Brazoria County • 25,703

Largest of the nine towns comprising the Brazosport industrial complex, Lake Jackson was established in the early 1940s by the Dow Chemical Company as an employee housing development. The company included four man-made lakes in its master plan for the community, which was built on a site that, before the Civil War, had been a plantation owned by Abner Jackson. These two factors led to the choice of town name.

LAKEVIEW
Panhandle • Hall County • 234

Deep Lake, which has since dried up, was visible from this point when settlers first came here. David H. Davenport founded Lakeview in 1908 and opened a combination store and post office, donated land for the construction of a cotton gin, and established the town's First State Bank.

LA MARQUE
Gulf Coast • Galveston County • 14,751 • luh MAHRK

Its earliest settlers called this place Highlands. But in the 1890s, the name was changed to La Marque, for the village of Lamarque in the Medoc region of southwestern France. Mrs. A. St. Ambrose, the French-born postmaster, suggested the name.

LAMESA

West Texas • Dawson County • 10,767 • luh-MEE-suh

Lamesa's name, Spanish for "the table," alludes to the area's location on the High Plains tableland of West Texas. Lamesa won a special election in 1905 to become the county seat, narrowly defeating Stemmons, a rival town. Soon afterward, residents of Stemmons moved their few homes and business places to Lamesa. A post office opened in Lamesa in 1904; the Stemmons post office, originally named "Chicago, Texas," closed in 1905.

LAMPASAS

Central Texas • Lampasas County • 7,881 • lam-PASS-uhs

Settled early in the 1850s, this community was called Burleson, but a legislative act in 1856 designated it as the Lampasas County seat and gave it the same name as the county. The county had been named for the Lampasas River, whose name is almost certainly a corruption of a Spanish word, perhaps *lampazos,* "water lilies."

LANCASTER

North central Texas • Dallas County • 23,550 • LANG-k's-ter

Abram Bledsoe, who settled here in 1847 on a tract of land he bought from Roderick Rawlins, laid out a townsite and named it for his former home town, Lancaster, Kentucky. After the Civil War, Bledsoe was elected county judge and later state comptroller.

LANGTRY

Southwest Texas • Val Verde County • 145

Originally known as Eagle Nest, the town that grew up here was named Langtry after a young civil engineer who worked the Galveston, Harrisburg & San Antonio rail line. But colorful Roy Bean, who arrived in 1885 and became the town's justice of the peace, named his saloon "The Jersey Lilly" for the famed English actress Lillie Langtry and claimed that the town was also named for her. In 1896, Judge Bean promoted a world championship prize fight between heavyweight boxers Bob Fitzsimmons of Australia and Peter Mahar of Ireland. At the time, the sport was illegal in Texas, but Bean sidestepped the law by holding the fight on a sandbar in the Rio Grande.

Roy Bean's saloon and courthouse in Langtry. Courtesy of Ray Miller.

LA PORTE
Southeast Texas • Harris County • 32,162

Settlers who emigrated from France arrived at this locale on upper Galveston Bay around 1889. The name they gave it means "the door," indicating that it would be a gateway to the sea. La Porte was a small village until mid-century when industrial development along the Gulf Coast, chiefly shipyards and petrochemical plants, spurred the town's growth.

LAREDO
South Texas • Webb County • 167,628 • luh-RAY-doh

Captain Tomas Sanchez, a Spanish army officer, founded this town in 1755. He named the settlement Laredo, for the coastal village in Spain that was the home town of his commanding officer, Colonel Jose de Escandon. The town passed from Spanish into Mexican and then into U.S. hands.

La Salle

Gulf Coast • Jackson County • 103

Rancher J. M. Bennett, Jr., subdivided a small part of his ranch and platted it as a townsite named Bennview in the early 1920s. In 1937, citizens of the community changed its name to La Salle, for the French explorer who in 1684 established his Fort St. Louis base at a location now widely believed to have been in Jackson County.

Latexo

East Texas • Houston County • 309 • luh-TECKS-oh

Latexo was named for the Louisiana & Texas Orchard company, which bought 3,000 acres of land here around 1901. The community, which had earlier been known as Stark's Switch, developed as a shipping point on the International & Great Northern rail line.

La Ward

Gulf Coast • Jackson County • 179

Established in 1904, this town was named for Lafayette Ward, a Jackson County native who operated a ranch here and helped to introduce Jersey, Hereford, and Brahman cattle to Texas.

Lazbuddie

Panhandle • Parmer County • 248 • LAZZ-buh-dih

Luther "Laz" Green and Andrew "Buddie" Sherley came to the Star Ranch here in 1924, bought a tract of land, and opened a store they called the Lazbuddie Commissary. The name was then given to the town that sprang up around the store.

League City

Gulf Coast • Galveston County • 39,931

Once the location of a Karankawa Indian village, this area attracted settlers who came by wagon from Louisiana in 1873 and called their community Clear Creek. The name was later changed to League City, in honor of a major landowner, John C. League.

LEAKEY
Southwest Texas • Real County • 447 • LAY-key

Pioneer settler John L. Leakey built a cabin here in 1857. The town named for him was founded in 1883 and chosen as the Real County seat in 1913.

LEANDER
Central Texas • Williamson County • 6,029

Leander was established in 1882 by the Austin & Northwestern Railroad when it constructed its tracks through this area. Leander "Catfish" Brown was an official of the railroad. Residents of Bagdad, a village bypassed by the rail line, abandoned their town and moved a mile east to Leander.

LELIA LAKE
Panhandle • Donley County • 125

This town and an adjacent creek, located along the Fort Worth & Denver Railroad, were named for Lelia Payne. Her brother-in-law, Judge G. A. "Gyp" Brown, founded the town in the late 1880s. When Donley County organized in 1882, Brown was designated as county judge. Later, after moving to Austin, he was appointed to the Texas Supreme Court, but died before taking the oath of office.

LEONA
East central Texas • Leon County • 223

Leona developed around the site of Moses Campbell's general store, opened in 1845. Some historians say the town and county names were chosen to honor early Texas colonizer Martin De Leon. Others say they were chosen for the region's yellow wolf, or "leon."

LEON VALLEY
South Texas • Bexar County • 10,502

Leon Valley, a suburban community ten miles from downtown San Antonio, was named for a Medina River tributary, Leon Creek, which flows nearby. The name of the creek itself, Spanish for "lion," came from the mountain lions sighted here by nineteenth-century pioneers. In 1952, when residents learned that San Antonio officials planned to annex this area, they quickly voted to incorporate Leon Valley instead.

LEVELLAND
Northwest Texas • Hockley County • 14,000

Cereal magnate C. W. Post bought the Oxsheer Ranch here in 1906 and, six years later, selected a tract of the land to be developed as the county seat. Post named the town Hockley City, but when an application for a post office was filed in 1922, postal officials rejected this and several other names. Post's widow and daughter then proposed a new name, Levelland—reflecting the area's level terrain—that won approval.

LEWISVILLE
North central Texas • Denton County • 69,200

Known first as Holford Prairie, this settlement was part of the historic Peters Colony and was named for two of the pioneer settlers, James and John Holford, who arrived in 1844. In the 1850s B. W. Lewis bought the Holford properties and renamed the town for himself. Lewisville has grown rapidly in recent decades, with expansion of Lake Lewisville, interstate highway construction, and development of Dallas-Fort Worth and Alliance airports.

LEXINGTON
Central Texas • Lee County • 1,088

James Shaw, a veteran of the Texas Revolution, was among the first settlers here after Texas won its independence from Mexico. He was the town's postmaster, as well as a school teacher and member of the state legislature. The town was known as a String Prairie until 1850, when residents voted to change the name to Lexington, after the historic Massachusetts town.

LIBERTY
Southeast Texas • Liberty County • 8,932

Several hundred Anglo-Americans settled here on a Spanish land grant in the 1820s. In 1831, Mexican land commissioner J. Francisco

Madero named the settlement Villa de la Santissima Trinidad de la Libertad (Town of the Most Holy Trinity of Liberty), which the English-speaking residents quickly shortened to Liberty. Some historians say the choice of the town name was influenced by early settlers who came to Texas from the vicinity of Liberty, Mississippi. After Texas won independence from Mexico, the town was incorporated and became the Liberty County seat. Its inland port provided regular water transport to and from Galveston Island and was a stopping point for steamers navigating the Trinity River. Sam Houston owned two plantation homes in the county and practiced law in Liberty between 1830 and 1850.

LIBERTY HILL
Central Texas • Williamson County • 300

W. O. Spencer, Taylor Smith, and George Barnes were among the settlers who arrived here in the 1840s and early 1850s. The settlement is said to have been named by Barnes for his home town in South Carolina's Kershaw County, or by Spencer, who became the first postmaster in 1853, or by anti-secessionist Smith who declared, "Liberty will rule my place!"

LILLIAN
Central Texas • Johnson County • 105

Driving a two-horse buggy one day in 1902, J. W. Cunningham arranged to spend the night here at the home of G. W. Renfro. During the visit, Cunningham bought some land from Renfro to develop as a townsite. Discovering while they negotiated that they each had a spouse named Lillian, they agreed to name the townsite for their wives.

LINN
Far south Texas • Hidalgo County • 450

Linn's development began when the Texas & New Orleans rail line established a station here in 1927 and Arcadio Guerra built a general store and cotton gin nearby. County Judge Walter M. Doughty named the town for his son, Linn, who was killed in a train accident at the age of 22. During the 1930s, the town was an important cattle-shipping point for the Rio Grande Valley.

LIPAN

Central Texas • Hood County • 427 • LYE-pan

T. A. Burns, who laid out this townsite in 1873 where the Palo Pinto and Granbury roads crossed, was the founder of Lipan. He named the town for the Lipan-Apache Indians, a Texas tribe that traveled great distances on hunting and warring expeditions.

LISSIE

Southeast Texas • Wharton County • 70

This community originally was named New Philadelphia by its first settlers, Walter Whitbread and Bryan Kelly, who arrived here in the mid-1870s, along with other immigrants leaving depressed economic conditions in Great Britain. In 1882, a school opened with Melissa Leveridge as teacher. When H. A. Adams was appointed postmaster several years later, he proposed that the post office's name be changed in her honor.

LITTLEFIELD

Northwest Texas • Lamb County • 6,386

Voters chose Littlefield as the new Lamb County seat in 1946, but its history began in 1913 when Arthur Duggan helped lay out the townsite and sell town lots. His wife named the town for her uncle, Major George W. Littlefield of Austin, a leading Texas rancher, cattleman, and banker. A store opened here that same year, and soon after a public library and the *Lamb County News* were established. Country music star Waylon Jennings was born in Littlefield in 1937.

LIVINGSTON

Southeast Texas • Polk County • 7,323

Moses Choate, who built a log cabin in this area in 1839, contributed 100 acres for the founding of this town, which later became the Polk County seat. He named Livingston for a town located near his former home in Sumter County, Alabama.

LLANO

Central Texas • Llano County • 3,267 • LAN-noh

Llano was named for the river traversing this county. The Spanish word *llano* means "plain" or "prairie" and probably refers to the West

Texas terrain where the Llano River has its source. German settlers arrived here in the 1840s to establish farms and raise livestock. In 1886, investors set off a speculative boom here, envisioning the area as a rich source of iron and precious metals. During the boom, a railroad line was built into Llano and the town's population swelled to an estimated ten thousand by 1893. Then the boom fizzled as miners found the mineral deposits were much less significant than they had been believed to be.

LOCKHART
South central Texas • Caldwell County • 9,925

Plum Creek was the original name of this community. It developed on land owned by Byrd Lockhart, who served with distinction in the Texas revolutionary army. The town changed its name to Lockhart and became the Caldwell County seat in 1848.

LODI
Northeast Texas • Marion County • 164 • LOH-dih

When a sawmill was built here in the 1870s, timber industry workers and their families formed this community on the Texas & Pacific rail line. A railroad worker, J. Lopresto, proposed the name Lodi after his home town in Italy.

LOLITA
Gulf Coast • Jackson County • 453 • lo-LEE-tuh

Founded in 1909, this town was named for Lolita Reese, whose grandfather, C. K. Reese, fought in the Texas Revolution. The townsite was platted on land that had been part of the Mitchell Ranch; two decades earlier the ranch had been fenced with the first barbed wire in Jackson County.

LOMETA
Central Texas • Lampasas County • 774 • loh-MEE-tuh

Originally called Montvale, Lometa was founded as a trading post on the Gulf, Colorado & Santa Fe Railway. When postal officials rejected Montvale as the name for the new town's post office, a sheep rancher suggested Lometa, apparently based on *lomita*, a Spanish word meaning "small hill." The town developed a business district over the years, but saloons were notably absent—the result of a resolution by early settlers to keep them out of town.

LONDON
Southwest Texas • Kimble County • 180

Horse trader Len Lewis moved to this area in 1878, got married, and developed a town on a tract of land he purchased. Robert Stevenson, father of future governor Coke R. Stevenson, established a general store in which a post office opened in 1882. Some say the town was named for London, England, while others contend it was named for a town in Laurel County, Kentucky.

LONE STAR
Northeast Texas • Morris County • 1,674

Lone Star began in the late 1930s as a residential community for workers at the Lone Star Steel Company mill. Like the company, the town derived its name from the single white star in the Texas state flag.

LONGVIEW
Northeast Texas • Gregg County • 75,271

Longview acquired its name in 1870, when the view from this site made an impression on surveyors planning a railroad route through the area. Three years later Longview became the Gregg County seat. The 1930 census counted about six thousand residents, a number that more than tripled soon afterward during the East Texas oil boom.

LOOP
New Mexico border • Gaines County • 315

Postal officials in Washington rejected Blue Goose and several other names proposed for the post office being opened here in 1912. Observing a cowboy twirling his lariat, someone suggested the name Loop, and it was accepted. Early settlers of Loop were mainly employees of the Double-Eye Quinn Ranch and other ranches in the area.

LOPENO
Far south Texas • Zapata County • 425 • loh-PEE-noh

The village of Lopeno was named for Fort Lopeno, built in 1821 by landowner Benito Ramirez as a combination fort, home, and chapel. In the early 1900s, Serafim Benavides established a general store in the town. The village relocated when Falcon Reservoir was created in 1952 and the original location was covered by the lake.

The Los Ebanos ferry. Courtesy of Ray Miller.

LOS EBANOS
Far south Texas • Hidalgo County • 100 • lohs EH-bah-nos

Early settlers from Mexico established Los Ebanos and named the town for two giant ebony trees overhanging the Rio Grande. One of the trees served as an anchor for the cable of the Los Ebanos Ferry, which by the 1990s was the last hand-powered, three-car ferry still operating on the river.

LOS FRESNOS
Far south Texas • Cameron County • 3,127 • lohs FREZ-nohs

Lon C. Hill, Sr., named this town Moseville in 1915, for his son, Lon Hill, Jr., often called "Mose." But the name soon was changed to Los Fresnos, after Rancho Los Fresnos, a ranch established in this area as early as 1770. Los Fresnos translates as "the ash trees."

LOVING
North central Texas • Young County • 300

Loving was founded in 1910 when the Gulf, Texas & Western Railroad constructed a line through Young County. The town was near the Goodnight-Loving Trail, a cattle drive route through New Mexico to Colorado that Oliver Loving and Charles Goodnight blazed in 1866. Loving also drove Texas cattle to market in Chicago and Denver. Thousands of others later rode the three routes that this "dean" of the cattle trail drivers pioneered.

LUBBOCK
Northwest Texas • Lubbock County • 194,202 • LUH-buhk

Like its county, this county seat was named for Thomas S. Lubbock, who fought for Texas independence, served as an army officer for the Republic of Texas, and later was a lieutenant colonel for Terry's Texas Rangers during the Civil War. His brother, Francis R. Lubbock, was governor of Texas from 1861 to 1863. Two communities, Monterey and Old Lubbock, consolidated in 1891 to form the township of Lubbock. Lubbock was later the birthplace of rock-and-roll legend Buddy Holly.

LUFKIN
East Texas • Angelina County • 32,590 • LUHF-kin

Lufkin was founded in 1882 as a station on the Houston, East & West Texas Railroad. There are two stories about the origin of the town name. One is that the railroad's president, Paul Bremond, named the town for his friend Abraham Lufkin, a Galveston cotton trader and city councilman. The other is that the town was named for Edwin P. Lufkin, the civil engineer who directed the railroad's survey of the area.

LULING
South central Texas • Caldwell County • 5,481 • LOO-ling

Luling developed from a small farming community into an established town in 1874 when the Galveston, Harrisburg & San Antonio line reached here. The town was named for Charles B. Luling, an investor in the railroad construction project. For two years, Luling was the terminus for the GH&SA line and gained a reputation as one of America's wildest, toughest towns until the railroad construction gangs moved elsewhere. A new period of hectic times and growth came after wildcatter Edgar B. Davis struck oil here in 1922.

LUMBERTON
Southeast Texas • Hardin County • 7,494

Lumberton was established around the turn of the century as a stop on the Gulf, Beaumont & Kansas City line, serving Hardin County's sawmills and logging camps.

MADISONVILLE
East Texas • Madison County • 4,222

This town was founded in 1853 and an early resident of the area suggested that it, like Madison County, be named in honor of President James Madison. After Madisonville became the county seat, a log courthouse was built in the center of town.

MALAKOFF
East Texas • Henderson County • 2,237 • MAL-uh-kawf

In the mid-1850s John Collins applied for a post office to be established in this community. He proposed the name Malakoff, after a place in Russia's Black Sea area often mentioned in news reports about the Crimean War. French forces succeeded in taking the Malakoff (or Malakov) tower, a key position, in early 1855, about six months before the Treaty of Paris ended hostilities.

MANCHACA
Central Texas • Travis County • 2,259 • MAN-sh'-kuh

This settlement southwest of Austin came into existence before the Civil War and grew a bit larger when it became a stop on the International & Great Northern Railroad in 1876. It was named for nearby Manchaca Springs. The springs derived their name, with a variation in spelling, from Jose Antonio Menchaca, a native of San Antonio who fought as an officer in the Texas revolutionary army.

MANSFIELD
North central Texas • Tarrant, Johnson, and Ellis counties • 23,400

The last names of two of this town's earliest settlers, Ralph S. Mann and Julian Feild, were combined and slightly altered to produce the name Mansfield. Around 1859, the two business partners built a steam-powered gristmill. Feild also opened a general store here. In the 1970s, growth of the Dallas-Fort Worth Metroplex turned this small town into a modern suburb.

MANVEL
Gulf Coast • Brazoria County • 4,794 • MAN-v'l

First settled in 1857 by William R. Booth and his wife, Elizabeth, this community attracted more residents after the Civil War. Its original name was Pamona. When the Gulf, Colorado & Santa Fe Railway reached Pamona and built a depot in 1880, the town's name was changed in honor of Allen Manvel, a veteran railroader who was later president of the Atchison, Topeka & Santa Fe. The town's economy was affected dramatically when Texaco struck oil here in 1931 and Manvel became one of South Texas' richest oil-producing areas.

MARATHON
Southwest Texas • Brewster County • 800

Marathon was established near the headquarters of the Circle Dot Ranch in 1882, when the Galveston, Harrisburg & San Antonio Railway reached this area. Albion Shepherd, a former sea captain working as a surveyor for the railroad, said the terrain between the mountains here in the Big Bend reminded him of Marathon, Greece.

MARBLE FALLS
Central Texas • Burnet County • 5,524

Adam Johnson, a cavalry general in the Civil War, developed and promoted Marble Falls in the 1880s. Johnson obtained a rail line for the town by persuading state legislators to fund construction of an Austin & Northwestern Railroad spur track through Marble Falls that would haul granite for the new state capitol building being constructed. The town was named for Colorado River waterfalls that poured over marble outcroppings. City officials were elected for the first time in 1907, and ten years later Marble Falls voters chose Orphelia Crosby Harwood as their mayor, reportedly the first woman mayor in the United States.

MARFA
Far west Texas • Presidio County • 2,557 • MAHR-fuh

 Located on a plateau between the Chisos Mountains, the Davis Mountains, and the Chinati Mountains, Marfa began in 1883 as a water stop on the Galveston, Harrisburg & San Antonio Railway. According to local lore, a railroad employee's wife named the town for Marfa, a character in the Dostoyevsky novel *The Brothers Karamazov*, which she had been reading.

MARLIN
Central Texas • Falls County • 6,561

In 1834, while Texas was still under Mexican rule, Sterling C. Robertson founded a colony in what is now Falls County and picked this site as his capital. Robertson, who later signed the Texas Declaration of Independence, named the town Sarahville de Viesca after his mother, Sarah, and Augustin Viesca, Mexican governor of Texas and Coahuila. John Marlin was alcalde, or administrative and judicial officer, of Robertson's colony, and in 1851 the town was renamed for him.

MARSHALL
Northeast Texas • Harrison County • 25,858

In 1842, three years after the first settlers arrived, Marshall became the seat of Harrison County. The town was established on land belonging to Peter Whetstone, who donated the courthouse square, streets, church and school sites, and 190 additional lots. Lawyer Isaac Van Zandt proposed that the town be named for John Marshall, chief justice of the U.S. Supreme Court from 1801 until 1835. Within two decades, Marshall was one of Texas's largest and most prosperous towns.

MASON
Central Texas • Mason County • 2,127

Mason grew up as a settlement around Fort Mason, a frontier fort established here in 1851 on a hill overlooking the Llano and San Saba rivers. Author Fred Gipson was born here in 1908 and wrote three novels, including *Old Yeller,* dealing with life near his home town.

MATADOR
Northwest Texas • Motley County • 726

H. H. "Hank" Campbell started the Matador ranch in the 1870s with A. M. Britton, his partner. In 1891, when Motley County was organized, Campbell used part of his land to establish a townsite. No other town then existed in Motley County, but to become the county seat, the new town of Matador still had to meet the legal requirement of having 20 businesses in operation. So Campbell had his cowboys set up the necessary number of businesses—for 24 hours. The plan worked, Matador became the county seat, and Campbell took office as the first county judge.

MATAGORDA
Gulf Coast • Matagorda County • 605 • mat-uh-GOHR-duh

Fifty-two pioneer families from New York and New England settled in Matagorda in 1825, after Stephen F. Austin obtained permission from Mexico to build a town at the mouth of the Colorado River. The town name means "thick shrubbery" or "dense bushes." Matagorda incorporated in 1830, became the county seat in 1837, and was an important gulf port for half a century.

An old lighthouse that once marked Half Moon Reef, Matagorda Bay. Courtesy of Ray Miller.

MATHIS
Gulf Coast • San Patricio County • 5,912

Thomas Henry Mathis, a Tennessee native, served in the Confederate Army, taught school in Arkansas, and became a rancher and entrepreneur while living on the Texas coast at Rockport. In 1887 Mathis gave the San Antonio & Aransas Pass Railway a right-of-way across his land and laid out a 300-acre townsite, named for himself, along the rail line.

MAYDELLE
East Texas • Cherokee County • 250

Development of this community started around 1906, while the Texas State Railroad was being constructed through the area. Local residents and merchants moved closer to the railroad, resulting in the consolidation of four rural communities—Java, Pine Town, Mount Comfort, and Ghent—at the townsite here. Governor Thomas M. Campbell's daughter, Maydelle, sang at a ceremony marking the opening of the townsite in 1910, and the town was named in her honor.

MAYPEARL
Central Texas • Ellis County • 891

The town of Eyrie was renamed Maypearl in 1903 when the International & Great Northern Railroad finished construction of its new rail line here. The town may have been named for May Pearl Trammel, wife of the railroad's chief engineer, or for the daughters of two railroad executives.

McALLEN
Far south Texas • Hidalgo County • 103,486

John McAllen, along with James Balli McAllen, John J. Young, Uriah Lott, and Lon C. Hill, incorporated the McAllen Townsite Company in late 1904, and the company established a townsite on the St. Louis, Brownsville & Mexico Railroad. Briggs & Smith, a Louisiana company, developed a rival townsite that became known as East McAllen. The original townsite was referred to as West McAllen. In 1911, citizens of the two McAllens voted to combine into a single town.

McCAMEY
West Texas • Upton County • 2,293

In 1925 George B. McCamey, partner in a Fort Worth drilling company, struck oil here. The driller persuaded the Kansas City, Mexico & Orient Railroad to build a switch and siding near the discovery well. Upon their completion, a railroad employee painted a sign that read "McCamey" and hung it on a boxcar, effectively naming the new boom town that had sprung up around the oil field. In three years' time, the town's population soared to between 10,000 and 12,000, with many workers living in hastily built "shotgun" houses.

McGregor
Central Texas • McLennan County • 4,855

McGregor developed in 1882 at the junction of the Gulf, Colorado & Santa Fe Railway and a narrow gauge line built by the St. Louis Southwestern Railroad. Town lots were first sold at a widely advertised auction conducted from a railroad flatcar. Many residents and merchants moved from Banks, a nearby village bypassed by the railroads. McGregor, called McGregor Springs in its early days, was named for Dr. G. C. McGregor of Waco, a retired physician who offered the Santa Fe a right-of-way through his property.

McKinney
North central Texas • Collin County • 38,700

McKinney was named for Collin McKinney, a signer of the Texas Declaration of Independence, land surveyor, legislator, and a leader in establishing the Disciples of Christ denomination in Texas. Settlers arrived here in the early 1840s. In 1848 voters made McKinney the new seat of Collin County, which like the town was named for Collin McKinney.

Memphis
Panhandle • Hall County • 2,457

This town's name came from a letter intended for someone in Memphis, Tennessee, but misaddressed to "Memphis, Tex." The Rev. J. W. Brice happened to see the wayward letter, marked "no such town in Texas," while in Austin around 1890. Brice was one of the partners developing a townsite here in the Panhandle and trying to decide upon a name for their new town and its post office. They chose Memphis.

Menard
Southwest Texas • Menard County • 1,595

Menard, originally called Menardsville, was established in 1858 near the ruins of Santa Cruz de San Saba, a Spanish mission which had been abandoned 101 years earlier. Menardsville became the seat of Menard

County in 1871. Its name was shortened in 1911 at the request of Fort Worth & Rio Grande railroad officials to make sign painting simpler. Both the town and county were named for Michel Branamour Menard, an Indian trader from Quebec, who founded the city of Galveston and signed the Texas Declaration of Independence.

MENTONE
New Mexico border • Loving County • 96

In 1893, a group of six men arrived here to form the Loving Canal & Irrigation Co. They organized Loving County, designated the settlement of Mentone—named by a surveyor for his faraway home town of Menton, France, but with an "e" appended—as county seat, and applied for a post office. Everything was abandoned three years later, including the county government and the town, when the irrigation promoters absconded with the money raised for the project. Mentone was re-established in the early 1930s, became the seat of Loving County again, and gained a population of 600, which then slipped below 100. Since mid-century, Loving County has consistently ranked as the nation's least populous county.

MERCEDES
Far south Texas • Hidalgo County • 14,762 • mer-SAY-deez

After development of this community began in 1904, the American Rio Grande Land & Irrigation Company, which owned the townsite, had trouble choosing a town name. After rejecting four other names, the company finally selected Mercedes, to honor the wife of Mexican president Porfirio Diaz.

MERIDIAN
Central Texas • Bosque County • 1,472

George B. Erath founded this town on July 4, 1854. Two years later, a post office opened with the name Meridian. County Commissioner J. N. Mabray proposed the name, perhaps because commissioners believed the town was located on the 98th meridian. Or the name may have come from nearby Meridian Creek, or two hills called Meridian Knobs.

MERIT

Northeast Texas • Hunt County • 215

Dr. O. Murcheson, who founded this community around 1870, wanted to call it Merritt, to honor a Judge Merritt. Others objected to naming the community for an individual. A compromise was reached with the name Merit.

MESQUITE

North central Texas • Dallas County • 116,350 • muh-SKEET

The Texas & Pacific Railway founded this town in 1873 as it built a station here on the rail line it was extending from East Texas to Dallas. The town was named after nearby Mesquite Creek. William Bradfield, who had earlier operated a stagecoach line, became the stationmaster, the first settler, and the first postmaster. In 1882, R. S. Kimbrough began publishing the weekly *Texas Mesquiter,* renamed *Mesquite News* about a century later. A farming community for most of its early history, Mesquite grew gradually until the late 1950s, when the pace of suburban home-building quickened and shopping center developer Gerri Von Froelich opened Big Town, one of the nation's first air-conditioned malls.

MEXIA

East central Texas • Limestone County • 6,801 • muh-HAY-uh

Mexia was founded along the Houston & Texas Central Railway line in 1871. A townsite company organized by the railroad offered lots for sale, and the town incorporated in 1873. It was named for Enrique Mexia—from whom the townsite company bought 1,920 acres to develop the town—and for Mexia's family. Enrique Mexia managed the vast estates that he and his sister, Adelaida, owned in Limestone, Anderson, and Freestone counties. He and his wife, the former Sarah Wilmer of Baltimore, and their daughter, Ynes, had moved to Limestone County in 1870.

MIAMI
Panhandle • Roberts County • 532

Miami was given an Indian name said to mean "sweetheart." The community originated in 1879 in the Red Deer Creek valley, at a stagecoach stop on the mail line between Mobeetie, Texas, and Las Vegas, New Mexico. A Southern Kansas Railway stop replaced the stagecoach stop in 1887. Voters chose Miami as the new Roberts County seat in an 1898 election. Parnell, the former county seat, was eventually abandoned by its residents, leaving Miami as the county's only town.

MIDLAND
West Texas • Midland County • 97,541

Midland was named for its location halfway between Fort Worth and El Paso. In 1881, during construction of its rail line between the two cities, the Texas & Pacific Railway built Midway Station, a section house, here. Ranchers moving into this area soon afterward called the location Midway, but—because other towns named Midway existed in Texas— the name was changed to Midland in 1884. Midland soon became a cattle ranching center and, after its First National Bank began business in 1890, a financial center as well. Its growth was spurred by discovery of oil in the surrounding Permian Basin in 1923.

MIDLOTHIAN
Central Texas • Ellis County • 6,850 • mid-LOH-thih-uhn

This community was first known as Hawkins Springs, presumably after William Allen Hawkins, who was issued a title to land here by the Peters Colony in 1848. In 1883 the Gulf, Colorado & Santa Fe Railroad extended its tracks to the town, which was renamed Midlothian at the suggestion of a train engineer who had emigrated to America from Midlothian County in Scotland.

MILAM
Louisiana border • Sabine County • 177 • MYE-l'm

Milam, once an Indian watering place, was settled in the late 1820s and called Red Mound. In 1835 it was renamed for a hero of the Texas war for independence, Ben Milam, who was slain by a sniper while leading a successful attack on Mexican army troops at San Antonio. When Texas was a republic, the town served as a port of entry for persons and goods crossing the Sabine River from Louisiana.

MILLICAN
Southeast Texas • Brazos County • 157

Millican was named for either Robert Millican or his son, Dr. Elliott Millican, or for both of these pioneer settlers who came to Brazos County in the 1820s. The community became a stagecoach stop and then, in 1860, the temporary terminus of the Houston & Texas Central Railway. At the outset of the Civil War, Millican was selected to be the location of a Confederate Army training camp. The town's population reached 3,000 in 1864, but diminished after a yellow fever epidemic and after businesses relocated to Bryan when the rail line built its tracks there.

MILLSAP
North central Texas • Parker County • 645

Tom and Dorcas Millsap's farm home was also a relay station on the stagecoach line between Weatherford and Palo Pinto in the 1870s. The family served meals to passengers while fresh horses were brought from a corral to replace tired ones. The stage line folded in 1880 when the Texas & Pacific Railway line was built. Three rural communities consolidated here at the railroad and chose Millsap as the town name.

MINEOLA
Northeast Texas • Wood County • 4,791 • min-ih-OH-luh

Major Ira Evans, an official of the International & Great Northern Railroad, combined the name of his daughter, Ola, with that of a friend, Minnie Patten, to name this town. Both the I&GN and the Texas & Pacific rail line reached Mineola in 1873. A town government formed that year and a post office opened, occupying a boxcar on the railroad tracks until another location became available.

MINERAL WELLS
North central Texas • Palo Pinto and Parker counties • 15,374

Judge J. A. Lynch and his family became this town's first settlers in 1877. Lynch is renowned in local history for founding this town and for discovering mineral water in the first well he dug. He credited it with curing his wife's rheumatism, and neighbors began drinking it for their

Mineral Wells during its early resort days. Courtesy of Houston Metropolitan Research Center, Houston Public Library.

ailments. Word spread that the mineral water could heal various maladies. Health seekers began arriving to drink and bathe in the water, and soon after the Texas & Pacific Railway reached the town in 1891, the first of several resort hotels was built. By the early 1920s, the town boasted 400 mineral wells. Visitors numbered between 100,000 and 150,000 a year, drawn by widely advertised resorts such as the Baker Hotel and Crazy Water Hotel. Carr P. Collins gained fame in the 1930s with his coast-to-coast radio broadcasts promoting Crazy Crystals, boxes of dehydrated minerals from the town's water.

MISSION
Far south Texas • Hidalgo County • 39,363

In 1861 Rene Guyard bequeathed a vast expanse of land to two members of a French religious order, the Missionary Oblates of Mary Immaculate, so that they could start a mission "for the propagation of the faith among the barbarians." John J. Conway and James W. Holt founded a town they called Mission in 1907 on 17,000 acres of land purchased from the order.

Missouri City

Southeast Texas • Fort Bend and Harris counties • 56,640

Houston land developers founded Missouri City in the 1890s. A promoter chose the name because advertising for the townsite was concentrated in the St. Louis area.

JUNE 29, 1996

HIDE TOWN STATION   MOBEETIE, TX 79061

Mobeetie

Panhandle • Wheeler County • 162 • moh-BEE-tee

This community first grew up around a supply store, established in 1874 by Bob Wright and Charles Rath at a buffalo hunters' camp on Sweetwater Creek. Most of the settlers soon relocated to a site several miles closer to Fort Elliott, an army post. At that time, a local historian says, the town was a rough and rowdy place with more than a dozen saloons "patronized by soldiers, buffalo hunters, freighters, gamblers, cowboys, and roughnecks of every description." When residents applied for a post office, they proposed the name Sweetwater. But when it turned out a Sweetwater post office already existed in Texas, they substituted the name Mobeetie, said by an Indian scout at Fort Elliott to mean "sweet water." Mobeetie became the county seat in 1879. But it later lost that status to the town of Wheeler after it was bypassed by the Santa Fe Railway and had suffered a tornado, two bank robberies, and another tornado.

MONAHANS
Far west Texas • Ward County • 7,851 • MAH-nuh-hanz

Originally called Monahan's Well, this town was named for T. J. "Pat" Monahan. He dug the first water well in this area and constructed a water tank here. Monahans became a stop on the Texas & Pacific Railway line and the town developed around it.

MOSCOW
Southeast Texas • Polk County • 170

David Griggs Green originally came to Texas to join Sam Houston's revolutionary soldiers. But he was delayed en route by floodwaters and arrived some days after the Battle of San Jacinto and the war's end. He founded this town in the 1840s and established a post office called Green's. Later, he suggested to postal officials that the name be changed to Greenville, but there was already a Greenville post office in Hunt County. The officials asked him for another name and he offered Moscow, the name of his home town in Tennessee, saying, "Moscow is so far away there will be no objection."

MOUNTAIN HOME
Southwest Texas • Kerr County • 96

The area is far from mountainous, but presumably the hills near his home gave Louis Nelson, this community's first postmaster, the idea of naming the post office Mountain Home. The name has been on the town's postmark since 1878, except for the three years when Aubrey Taylor was postmaster. Taylor persuaded officials to rename the post office for his wife, Eura, but Olive Estes, who succeeded Taylor in 1924, had the name changed back to Mountain Home.

MOUNT CALM
Central Texas • Hill County • 326

Mount Calm took shape as a scattered settlement in the 1850s. The settlers relied on the skills of a French blacksmith and wheelwright named Montcalm, and they gave an anglicized version of his name to their village and its post office in 1858.

MOUNT ENTERPRISE
East Texas • Rusk County • 534

This community was originally known as Mulberry Grove. In 1849 it changed its name to Mount Enterprise, in recognition of a small hill nearby and the business enterprises of some of its citizens, particularly Charles Vinson and his brother. The Vinsons operated a shop that made furniture, wagons, buggies, and caskets.

MOUNT PLEASANT
Northeast Texas • Titus County • 13,795

Ancient tribes constructed a great mound near the red mineral springs in this area. Centuries later, the Caddo Indians called the site "pleasant mound," a name that evolved into Mount Pleasant. This town was founded as the Titus County seat in 1846.

MOUNT VERNON
Northeast Texas • Franklin County • 2,522

A post office opened in 1848 to serve settlers in this area. Stephen Keith, who became the postmaster, contributed land for the development of a townsite. The community that grew up here was first called Keith and then Lone Star. Later, the name became Mount Vernon, after George Washington's home. In the late 1890s, two weekly newspapers were published here, the *Franklin Herald* and the *Mount Vernon Optic;* they merged to become the *Mount Vernon Optic-Herald* in 1906.

MUENSTER
Oklahoma border • Cooke County • 1,499 • MUNS-ter

August and Emil Flusche founded Muenster in 1889 as a German Catholic colony, promoting it to German immigrants who had settled in the Midwest. The town, named for the capital of Westphalia, incorporated in 1927, with Ben Hellman as the first mayor and "burgermeister."

MULESHOE
New Mexico border • Bailey County • 4,453

Muleshoe was founded in 1913, when the Pecos & Northern Texas Railway tracks reached this area, and became the Bailey County seat four years later. The town took its name from the Muleshoe Ranch, headquartered nearby, which was part of Charles and Ed Warren's cattle empire. The War- rens first bought 40,000 acres from the giant XIT Ranch and later increased their holdings to 150,000 acres. Their Muleshoe Ranch became the most famous of several ranches of the same name in Texas. The town of Muleshoe was incorporated in 1926. On its main street is the National Mule Memorial, unveiled on the Fourth of July, 1965.

Nacogdoches
East Texas • Nacogdoches County • 32,776 • nak-uh-DOH-chis

The historic town of Nacogdoches is named for the Nacogdoche Indi- ans, a Caddo tribe, and archeologists have found evidence of Indian set- tlements dating back to the thirteenth century at this site. French explor- er La Salle arrived here in 1687, and the Spanish established a mission, Nuestra Senora de Guadalupe de los Nacogdoches, in 1716. A settlement grew up in the vicinity of the mission in the 1780s and eventually became a center of unrest, dissent, and revolutionary activity. It was a gateway for volunteers from southern states who came to join the revolution against Mexico. Soon after the founding of the Texas republic, the town of Nacogdoches incorporated and formed a municipal government.

Nada
Southeast Texas • Colorado County • 165 • NAY-duh

This town's first settlers, the J. W. Schoellmann family, arrived in early 1871. Other families soon followed, mostly Czechs and Germans coming from elsewhere in Colorado County. A post office named Vox Populi— Latin for "voice of the people"—opened after Frank Frnka established a general store in 1882. Twelve years later, the village and its post office took the new name Nada, an adaptation of *nadja,* the Czech word for "hope."

Natalia
Southwest Texas • Medina County • 1,366 • nuh-TAL-yuh

The Medina Irrigation Company founded Natalia in 1912. It was named after Natalie Pearson, but her name was misspelled on the appli- cation for a town post office. Several years later, she married the business manager of the *London Times,* Reginald Nicholson, and lived the rest of her life in England. Natalie was the daughter of Dr. Fred Stark Pearson, chief engineer for the Medina Dam project and the 35,000-acre irriga- tion district in Medina, Atascosa, and Bexar counties.

NAVASOTA

Southeast Texas • Grimes County • 7,026 • nav-uh-SOH-tuh

Pioneers crossed Louisiana and settled at this bend of the Navasota River as early as the 1820s. The river's name, which the town also adopted, may have been a corruption of the Indian name for the river, variously recorded as Nabatsoto or Nabototo. Or it may have a Spanish origin, referring to the "nativity of de Soto." In the 1860s, Navasota gained importance as a trade and shipping center. The town acquired a telephone system by 1885 and added electric lights and a water system in the early 1890s.

NAZARETH

Panhandle • Castro County • 309

Father Joseph Reisdorff moved here in 1902 with four Catholic families, establishing a colony that he named Nazareth, after the biblical town. Other settlers were attracted by advertisements Father Reisdorff placed in out-of-state newspapers. The village developed as a farming community with a largely German Catholic population.

NECESSITY

North central Texas • Stephens County • 10

When residents of a location known as Cottonplant applied for a post office in 1893, they sought to convince Washington officials that one was badly needed by proposing to name it Necessity. Necessity's population reached 100 by 1910 and later jumped to an estimated 800 during the oil boom at nearby Ranger and Breckenridge.

NECHES

East Texas • Anderson County • 175 • NAY-chis

When the International & Great Northern Railroad built its tracks through this area in 1872, a town developed here called Nechesville, later shortened to Neches. The name came from the nearby Neches River, which in turn received its name from the Neche Indians, who lived along the river during the seventeenth and eighteenth centuries.

A replica Dutch windmill in Nederland. Courtesy of Ray Miller.

NEDERLAND
Southeast Texas • Jefferson County • 16,620 • NEE-der-l'nd

Immigrants from the Netherlands ("Nederland" in Dutch) founded this town in 1897, settling at a townsite established near Beaumont by the Port Arthur Townsite Company and Port Arthur Land Company. The land company built the Orange Hotel to provide living quarters for the Dutch families until they had built their own houses. The newcomers held a community celebration on September 8, 1898, the coronation day of Queen Wilhelmina in the old country. The Dutch immigrants established rice and dairy farms, but discovery of the Spindletop oil field nearby in 1901 made oil refining and related petrochemical industries the town's economic base.

NEEDVILLE
Southeast Texas • Fort Bend County • 3,241

This town's first settler, August Schendel, built a home here in 1891, proceeded to build a general store and a cotton gin, and then applied for a town post office. As a joke, he proposed the name Needmore, to convey the idea that the community needed more of everything. Since Texas already had a post office named Needmore, postal officials changed the name to Needville. After Schendel laid out a townsite and began selling lots in 1898, Needville started to get some of the things it needed: more stores, two schools, several churches, another cotton gin, an electric power plant, railroad access, a bank, and a movie theater were all added within two decades.

NEMO
Central Texas • Somervell County • 56

Nemo was originally known as Johnson Station, for Jimmie Johnson, an early settler who arrived here with his family in a covered wagon in 1858. Years later, an application for a post office was sent to Washington with the request that it be named for Jimmie Johnson. A postal official sent word back that a shorter name was needed. According to a local historian, A. R. Rinker, proprietor of the general store and Johnson's son-in-law, declared, "If Jimmie Johnson's name isn't good enough for the post office, no one's is." A school teacher then suggested Nemo, explaining it was a Latin word meaning "nobody." Another local legend has it instead that, on a whim, Rinker proposed Nemo because it rhymed with the names of two other post offices, Rainbow and Bono, on the mail route from Glen Rose to Cleburne.

NEVADA
North central Texas • Collin County • 655 • nuh-VAY-duh

Granville Stinebaugh moved from Missouri to Texas in 1870 and bought 160 acres of farmland in southeastern Collin County. The town of Nevada developed on Stinebaugh's land and was named for his former home town in Vernon County, Missouri.

NEWARK
North central Texas • Wise and Tarrant counties • 818 • NOO-erk

This community was known informally by several different names, including Caddo Village, Sueville, Huff Valley, and Ragtown, until the 1860s, when it became Odessa and had an operating post office. That post office then closed for almost three decades. The Chicago, Rock Island & Texas Railroad reached here in 1893. When railroad officials obtained permission to re-open the post office, they also renamed it, and the town, after New Jersey's largest city, Newark.

NEW BOSTON
Arkansas border • Bowie County • 5,119

In the 1830s, settlers established a Bowie County town named Boston, after W. J. Boston, proprietor of the first general store. Boston's merchants persuaded officials of the Texas & Pacific Railway to develop a townsite along the rail line, four miles from the existing town, in 1876. By the following year, many of Boston's merchants and residents had moved to the new site, where a post office was established with the name New Boston. The original town became known as Old Boston.

NEW BRAUNFELS
South central Texas • Comal County • 35,290 • noo BRAHN-f'lz

New Braunfels was established in 1845 at a site on Comal Creek selected by Prince Carl of Solms-Braunfels, commissioner general of the Adelsverein organization. Inspired by what he had read about Texas, Prince Carl founded the organization, which established colonies in the new Texas republic and sponsored the emigration of German artisans and peasants to inhabit them. Nicolaus Zink led the first wagontrain of German settlers to the site, where the arriving families received town lots and ten-acre farm plots. The settlement was named for Braunfels, Prince Carl's ancestral castle on the Lahn River in the German state of Wurt-

SECOND ANNUAL

Hummel

FEST ™

NEW BRAUNFELS, TX. 78130

HUMMEL FEST STATION
MAY '20 1994

temberg. By 1850, New Braunfels was estimated to be the fourth largest town in Texas and well on its way to being a successful farming and ranching center.

NEW CANEY
Southeast Texas • Montgomery County • 2,771

Austin and Sarah Presswood settled in 1862 on this site near Caney Creek, which contained thickets of cane plants. Presswood was what later settlers called the community that formed here. Around 1877, the Houston, East & West Texas Railway built a depot named Caney Station in the town. When a post office opened in 1882, it was given the name New Caney.

NEWCASTLE
North central Texas • Young County • 547

The Belknap Coal Company began mining here in 1908. Samuel Hardy is credited with proposing that the town's post office, which opened that same year, be named Newcastle after the English town New-castle-upon-Tyne, famed for its coal mines since the thirteenth century.

NEW DEAL
Northwest Texas • Lubbock County • 651

Monroe was the original name of this town, a farming community founded in 1909 and named for local landowner Monroe Abernathy. When Monroe's school district combined in 1935 with three small neighboring districts, it took the name New Deal School District, in tribute to President Franklin Roosevelt's social and economic programs. The town also changed its name from Monroe to New Deal when its post office opened in 1949.

New Home
Northwest Texas • Lynn County • 205

New Home developed at the turn of the century when the Deuce of Hearts Ranch opened its land for settlement and a few homes and a church were built. Settler L. G. DePriest suggested the name New Home because "this place is a new home for all of us."

Newton
Louisiana border • Newton County • 1,918

The Texas Legislature created Newton County in 1846 and named it in honor of Sergeant John Newton, who fought in the American revolutionary army. The town of Newton was established in 1853 at the geographic center of the county. Residents built a courthouse to trump the leaders of rival Burkeville in an ongoing struggle over which town would be the county seat.

New Ulm
Southeast Texas • Austin County • 650

James C. Duff established this community on a tract of land he bought in 1841. It was known as Duff's Settlement until 1852, when a post office opened under the name New Ulm. The name was proposed by immigrants who came to Texas from the German state of Wurttemberg, where Ulm has been a commercial center since the Middle Ages and is now famous as the birthplace of Albert Einstein. In the 1850s, New Ulm's business district included a cigar factory, three cabinet shops, and three breweries.

New Waverly
Southeast Texas • Walker County • 1,048

Families from Alabama settled the community of Waverly in the 1850s. It was probably named for Sir Walter Scott's popular Waverly novels. In 1870 residents rejected the International & Great Northern Railroad's request for a right-of-way through the town, so the railroad bypassed Waverly and established a station ten miles west that became known as New Waverly. After Waverly residents began to move to the new site, the town they left behind was soon called Old Waverly.

NOBILITY
Oklahoma border • Fannin County • 21

Established a short time before the Civil War, this village was named for William Gentry, an early settler. But postal officials in Washington rejected Gentry as a name for the town post office in 1881. So residents chose the substitute name Nobility.

NOCONA
Oklahoma border • Montague County • 3,158 • noh-KOH-nuh

A community called Jordanville existed here in the mid-1880s, named for rancher D. J. Jordan. After officials turned down Jordanville as a name for the town's post office, a Texas Ranger is credited with the idea of naming this town for Peta Nocona. The Comanche leader was the husband of Cynthia Ann Parker—who was abducted as a child from her frontier home and later fully assimilated into Comanche life—and father of Chief Quanah Parker.

NOLAN
West central Texas • Nolan County • 47

This village formed in 1928 when two communities, Old Nolan and Dora, consolidated at a midway point on Farm Road 126. Both communities had been founded around 1890. Old Nolan was named for Nolan County, which in turn was named for Philip Nolan, an Irish-American adventurer slain by Spanish troops in 1801. They intercepted him while he was leading an expedition in central Texas to capture wild horses. (Nolanville in Bell County is also a namesake of Nolan's.) Dora took its name for Dora Collings Rhodes, daughter of the community's first postmaster. When the two communities merged, their schools formed a consolidated district named, oddly, Divide.

NOME
Southeast Texas • Jefferson County • 443

There are several stories about the origin of Nome's name. The most widely accepted one is that the town was named in 1903 after Nome, Alaska. Residents of Sour Lake Junction, as this place was previously known, could easily draw a comparison between the 1900 Alaskan gold rush and the oil boom taking place in their own area in 1902 and 1903. Another story concerns a map of the region drawn by a cartographer who did not know what this town was called, and wrote "Name?" on the map. The printer, it is said, misread the word as "Nome."

NORMANGEE
East central Texas • Leon and Madison counties • 729 • NOHR-m'n-jee

Construction of two railroads through this area attracted many settlers from the nearby Rogers Prairie community and resulted in the founding of Normangee. The Houston & Texas Central arrived first and established a station in 1905, followed two years later by the Trinity & Brazos Valley Railway. Normangee was named for Judge Norman Goree Kittrell of Houston, who served the 61st Judicial District from 1903 to 1913. The town incorporated in 1913, disincorporated in 1917, and reincorporated in 1919.

NORMANNA
South Texas • Bee County • 75

Two settlements in this vicinity have contributed significantly to Normanna's history—one, a community called San Domingo, established by pioneers around 1850, and the second, a colony of Norwegian immigrants, founded about two miles away in 1892. When the San Antonio & Aransas Pass Railway extended its line to the second site in 1896, San Domingo residents moved there. Normanna is a Norwegian word meaning "one from the north" or "far north."

NOTREES
West Texas • Ector County • 338 • NOH-treez

Notrees derived its name from the most distinguishing feature of its terrain: the absence of trees. C. J. Brown built a retail store here in 1946 to serve the adjacent TXL Oil Field. He proposed the name when he applied for a post office to be established at his store. Later, residents changed the landscape by planting shade trees.

NOVICE
Central Texas • Coleman County • 189 • NAH-vis

Two brothers, Will and Joe Fletcher, opened a general merchandise store in the 1880s and sought approval to open a post office there. Since they were novices at operating a business, they proposed Novice as the post office name.

NURSERY
Gulf Coast • Victoria County • 260

Gilbert Onderdonk was a pioneer in the scientific study and cultivation of fruit in Texas. When the San Antonio & Mexican Gulf Railroad built its line through cattleman W. H. "Uncle Billy" Kyle's vast landholdings in the early 1880s, Kyle persuaded the prominent fruit grower to locate a branch of his nursery business here and use the railroad as a shipping point. Onderdonk established a townsite he called Nursery and opened a post office so that he could expand his mail-order business.

OAKLAND
Southeast Texas • Colorado County • 80

The community of Prairie Point had its application for a post office denied in 1857. Postmaster Amasa Turner offered to relocate his post office from Lavaca County to this town on the condition that its name remain Oakland, for the home of David G. Burnet, who served as interim president of the Republic of Texas during the revolution in 1836. When the post office moved here, Prairie Point changed its name to Oakland.

ODEM
Gulf Coast • San Patricio County • 2,702

When the St. Louis, Brownsville & Mexico Railway extended its tracks here in 1907, this county's colorful and popular sheriff, David Odem, arranged for a 110-acre townsite to be platted at the railroad's flag stop. New residents bought town lots and a post office opened in 1909. The town was named for Sheriff Odem, whose career included cattle ranching, operating a general store at Sinton, co-founding the *San Patricio County News,* and dealing extensively in real estate. Odem absorbed the nearby communities of Sharpsburg, Angelita, Meansville, and Kaleta, and it incorporated in 1928.

ODESSA
West Texas • Ector County • 94,518

After the Texas & Pacific Railway completed its tracks across West Texas in 1881, land promoters in Zanesville, Ohio, envisioned the money they could make by promoting a new town at this location on the rail line. According to local lore, the site was named by railroad construction workers from Russia, who said the wide, flat prairie reminded them of the steppes, or semi-arid plains, surrounding Odessa in the Ukraine. From 1886 to 1888, the Ohio promoters sent prospective buyers on excursion trains to Texas, promising them "pure water, sunshine, and no mosquitoes." Some of the prospects settled at Odessa, but a drought hindered the sales campaign and the land promoters declared bankruptcy. Odessa, however, grew steadily if not spectacularly. It was chiefly a trade center for ranchers until the late 1920s, then became the Permian Basin's oil field supply and service depot and a regional trucking center. Drilling equipment made in Odessa was soon marketed worldwide.

OILTON
South Texas • Webb County • 585

In 1922, when oil was discovered in this vicinity, a post office opened here with a new, petroleum-inspired name. The small settlement that had existed at this location for several decades was previously named Torrecillas. Its name referred to the "little towers"—two local rock formations.

OKLAUNION
Oklahoma border • Wilbarger County • 138 • ohk-luh-YOON-y'n

About 1888, Joe "Buckskin" Works gave the town of Mayflower a new name, Oklaunion. Works hoped that the Fort Worth & Denver City Railway and the Frisco Line, which provided rail service to Oklahoma, would establish a junction here. The two lines did later establish a junction, but at Vernon instead of Oklaunion.

OLD GLORY
Northwest Texas • Stonewall County • 125

In the early 1900s, farmers of German descent moved to this area and established a townsite they called Brandenburg. Several years later, the Swenson Land & Cattle Company created a second townsite two miles away, which was given the name New Brandenburg. When war broke out in Europe in 1914 and public sentiment against Germany grew, residents of the combined Brandenburg community decided to change the town name to reflect their American patriotism. The new name, Old Glory, became official on Flag Day, June 14, 1918.

Old Ocean

Gulf Coast • Brazoria County • 915

This town was named about 1935 for the Old Ocean field, where legendary oilman James S. Abercrombie of Houston had discovered oil a short time earlier. Soon after Pearl Harbor Day, President Franklin Roosevelt asked Abercrombie and his partner, Dan Harrison, to build an aviation fuel refinery at the Old Ocean field. Construction and operation of the plant boosted the town's population. The name Old Ocean came from a geologist's determination that the area had, many millennia before, been undersea.

Olney

North central Texas • Young County • 3,347 • AHL-nih

After settlers began arriving here in 1879, land for a townsite was donated by John Groves. David Penn, publisher of the *Olney Enterprise,* cites three stories about the origin of the town name: Olney was named after Congressman Richard Olney for his help in getting a post office established; John Groves named Olney after an assistant postmaster general; or Groves named Olney after the seat of Richland County in Illinois.

Omaha

Northeast Texas • Morris County • 970

Thompson Morris established a townsite at this location in 1880, and the settlers who moved here called the place Morristown. But postal officials gave the town's post office the name Gavett. On a Saturday afternoon in 1886, seven citizens decided to replace both names. They each wrote down a suggestion, then placed the slips of paper in a hat and drew one. The name drawn was Omaha, said to have been jotted down by a Hugh Ellis who had lived in a rural Alabama community by that name.

Onalaska

Southeast Texas • Polk County • 995 • uhn-uh-LAS-kuh

Veteran lumberman William Carlisle decided in 1904 to establish his third sawmill here, and assigned one of his Carlisle Lumber Company employees to get the operations under way. Because his first sawmill was in Onalaska, Wisconsin, and the second in Onalaska, Arkansas, Carlisle named this place Onalaska as well.

ORANGE

Louisiana border • Orange County • 19,212

In 1858, the Texas Legislature changed this town's name from Madison to Orange, since it was the Orange County seat. Local historians say that Orange County may have acquired its name from orange groves in the vicinity. It was more likely named after Orange, New Jersey, the home town of A. H. Reading. Reading was one of three commissioners appointed to organize the county in 1852.

ORCHARD

Southeast Texas • Fort Bend County • 524

After the Gulf, Colorado & Santa Fe Railway built its route through this area, Dr. C. H. Chenoweth, Frank Chenoweth, and T. W. Aylor were among the first to move to the townsite established here. Each planted a large orchard on his property, inspiring the name given to the local post office in 1892. But the hurricane of 1900 wiped out the fruit trees, and settlers turned to raising cotton, corn, and livestock instead.

OVALO

West central Texas • Taylor County • 225 • oh-VAL-uh

The Spanish word meaning "oval" became this town's name because of its location in an oval-shaped valley. The Abilene & Southern Railway Company and its stockholders controlled ownership of the townsite established here. Lots were placed on sale in 1909 and growth came quickly to the town, bringing a bank and more than 50 other business enterprises during its first five years.

OZONA

Southwest Texas • Crockett County • 3,477 • oh-ZOH-nuh

Land surveyor E. M. Powell founded this town, first known as Powell Well, in 1891. He installed a windmill at the water well he dug here, and his agent, Joe Moss, sold lots to prospective settlers. Voters chose Powell Well as the county seat over Emerald, the county's only other town. Powell then proposed renaming the town Ozona to reflect its clear skies and fresh air. As many of Emerald's residents moved to Ozona, often taking their houses and other buildings with them, that settlement eventually disappeared, and Ozona became the only town in Crockett County.

PADUCAH

Northwest Texas • Cottle County • 1,668 • puh-DOO-kuh

Paducah owes its name to Paducah, Kentucky, a city named for Chief Paduke of the Chickasaw tribe. One of the former Kentuckians who settled here was E. E. Biggs, who offered free land to settlers if they supported naming the town Paducah and making it the county seat. Biggs was successful on both counts: Paducah became the seat of Cottle County in 1892.

PAINT ROCK

Central Texas • Concho County • 214

This county seat took the name Paint Rock from a remarkable display of stone-age Indian art, just two miles away. Some 1,500 pictographs are painted along a half-mile limestone canyon wall.

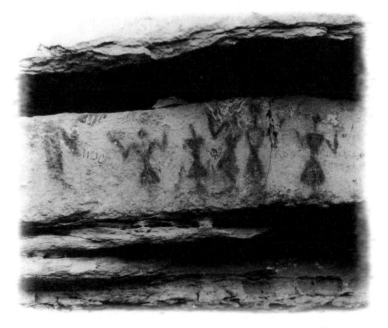

The ancient rock art at Paint Rock. Courtesy of Ray Miller.

PALACIOS

Gulf Coast • Matagorda County • 4,515 • puh-LASH-uhs

Palacios was named for its location on Tres Palacios Bay, which translates from Spanish as "three palaces." In 1901, the Texas Rice Development Company bought part of a bull pasture from the estate of rancher Abel Head "Shanghai" Pierce and developed it as a townsite. The company paid a bonus to the New York, Texas & Mexico Railroad to extend its tracks to Palacios.

PALESTINE

East Texas • Anderson County • 18,239 • PAL-uhs-teen

Palestine was founded in 1846 and named for Palestine, Illinois, the former home of Daniel Parker. An ordained minister and leader in the Primitive Baptist church, Parker resided in Anderson County at the time of his death in 1844.

PALMER

Central Texas • Ellis County • 1,870

The Houston & Texas Central Railway held ceremonies on the day in 1872 when its first train arrived here. The keynote speaker for the occasion was Dr. D. S. Palmer, a Houston physician and railway stockholder, who spoke so eloquently that his listeners decided to name the town for him.

PALO PINTO

North central Texas • Palo Pinto County • 411 • pa-loh PIN-toh

Texas legislators created Palo Pinto County in 1856 and directed that a county seat be established in or near its center. The legislative act assigned the county seat the name Golconda, after an ancient city in India famed in legend for its riches. In 1858, the town was renamed Palo Pinto. The Spanish name may refer to spotted oak trees in the area or, translated as "painted post," may refer to petrified wood in the Brazos River Valley.

PAMPA

Panhandle • Gray County • 19,760 • PAM-puh

Pampa was given its name by George Tyng, manager of the White Deer Lands Trust and the Diamond F Ranch, who moved his headquarters here around the turn of the century. He said this area reminded him of Argentina's pampas, or plains, which he had once visited.

Pancake
Central Texas • Coryell County • 11

Pancake was named in 1884 for this rural village's first postmaster, John R. Pancake. Population thereafter became so small that the town has not had a post office of its own since 1908.

Pandora
South Texas • Wilson County • 125

In the late 1890s, when this village became a stop on the San Antonio & Gulf Railroad, it was given the name Pandora. As is the case with towns called Pandora in other states, there seems to have been no special reason why the Greek mythological figure's name was chosen.

Panna Maria
South Texas • Karnes County • 96 • pan-uh muh-REE-uh

Panna Maria, meaning "Virgin Mary," is believed to be the oldest continuing Polish settlement in America and the location of the nation's oldest Polish church and school. The town was founded in 1854 by Polish families who had been encouraged by a young Catholic missionary, Father Leopold Moczygemba, to leave Prussian-dominated Upper Silesia and establish a colony on the Texas frontier. In 1856, the settlers started school classes in a barn, established the Panna Maria post office, and built and consecrated the Immaculate Conception Church. The church moved to its present building in 1877. An estimated ten thousand people gathered at the church for a 1966 mass and barbecue, held to mark the millennium of Polish Christianity.

Panola
Louisiana border • Panola County • 296 • pan-OH-luh

This village's first name was Latex, because of its location about four miles west of the Louisiana-Texas state line. The community developed when a natural gas company found a gas field here in 1924 and built houses and other facilities for its employees. The name Panola comes from the Cherokee word *ponolo,* "cotton."

PARADISE

North central Texas • Wise County • 275

Bill Anderson's general store, built in the early 1870s, was the center of the community that developed here. The town was first known as Eldorado, then as New Town, Old Paradise, Old Town, and finally Paradise Prairie, shortened to Paradise when a post office opened in 1876. W. L. Burress is said to have suggested the name because the area's natural beauty and abundant wildflowers made it "a paradise on earth."

PARIS

Northeast Texas • Lamar County • 25,182

The successor to a settlement called Pinhook, this town was founded in 1844 on land that merchant George W. Wright donated for the establishment of a Lamar County seat. T. H. R. Poteet, an employee of Wright, named the town for Paris, France.

PASADENA

Southeast Texas • Harris County • 132,929

Banker and real estate investor John H. Burnett founded Pasadena in 1893. It was named for Pasadena, California, which had taken its name from a Chippewa word meaning "valley between the hills." The new town began to develop in 1894, when the LaPorte, Houston & Northern short-line railroad built its tracks here. After area farms were devastated by the 1900 Galveston hurricane, the American Red Cross supplied them with 1.5 million strawberry plants. Pasadena soon became a center for the production of strawberries and other fruits and vegetables. Its economic base shifted mid-century as oil refineries and war-related industrial plants opened along the Houston Ship Channel.

PATTISON
Southeast Texas • Waller County • 378

According to local lore, this village's name came about in the mid-nineteenth century, as a result of a bet between two plantation owners. They held a race for the privilege of having this place named for the winning horse's owner, and James Pattison's horse won. Getting Pattison's name spelled correctly was not, however, a matter so quickly resolved. A post office opened in 1879 with the name Patterson's Station, changed in 1883 to Patterson, and at last, in 1916, to Pattison.

PAWNEE
South Texas • Bee County • 249

Fred Hoff and his family were the first settlers in this vicinity, arriving near the turn of the century. Other families arrived in the early 1900s. The settlers are said to have named their community Pawnee after finding a board, with the Indian tribe's name burned into it, nailed to a tree in the vicinity, apparently by a passing traveler. Two local historians believe a young man, nostalgic for his former home in Pawnee County, Kansas, mounted the sign. Another believes it was placed by someone who had found Pawnee arrowheads in nearby Sulphur Creek.

PEARLAND
Gulf Coast • Brazoria County • 26,604 • PAIR-land

Pearland was established in 1882 at a siding switch on the Gulf, Colorado & Santa Fe Railway. A post office named Mark Belt opened in 1883, but within the year changed its name to Pearland, because of the abundance of pear trees in the area. Before the first decade of the twentieth century, two general stores and other businesses opened in the town. The 1900 hurricane that devastated Galveston destroyed fruit trees and caused other damage here, but Pearland recovered. Since the 1950s, growth of the Houston area has caused the town's population to rise rapidly.

PEARSALL
South Texas • Frio County • 7,864 • PEER-sahl

The International & Great Northern Railroad founded Pearsall in 1882 on a 2,000-acre tract of land it acquired here. The town was named for Thomas W. Pearsall, vice president of the railroad. Residents and merchants of Frio Town, a community bypassed by the railroad, moved to Pearsall and temporarily occupied tents clustered around the depot.

PECOS

West Texas • Reeves County • 11,542 • PAY-kuhs

The Texas & Pacific Railway came here in 1881, encouraged by landowner George Knight's offer of a depot site. The railroad's arrival provided the impetus for development of this town, named for its location on the Pecos River, a major tributary of the Rio Grande. Only two years after being founded, Pecos became the scene of what may have been the world's first rodeo when, competing against cowboys from two other ranches, foreman Trav Windham of the Lazy Y roped and tied a steer on Oak Street in 22 seconds. The town's population was estimated at 150 in 1885, when it was reputed to have more saloons per capita than any other place in Texas. Pecos later developed into a center for oil production and for growing and marketing gourmet cantaloupes. Madison L. Todd of Pecos was called the Cantaloupe King during the 1930s, 1940s, and 1950s, when he shipped perfectly ripened melons via Railway Express to points as far as 1,500 miles away.

PENITAS

Far south Texas • Hidalgo County • 1,388 • puh-NEE-tuhs

Penitas, which means "little pebbles," was the name given to this settlement in its early days because of nearby gravel deposits. According to local lore, the settlement originated with a group of Spaniards who were part of the ill-fated Panfilo de Narvaez expedition of 1520. Although the claim has not been authenticated, it is believed here that Penitas is one of the oldest towns in the United States.

PENWELL

West Texas • Ector County • 74 • PIN-wel

In October 1929, J. H. Penn drilled a discovery well southwest of Odessa that began flowing with an output so great that tanks with a capacity of 9,500 barrels quickly filled and emergency arrangements were required. The town of Penwell, named for Penn's well, was established a month later and grew as drilling expanded. Its population was estimated at 3,000 during the height of the field's oil production in the 1930s. Businesses included lumber yards, clothing stores, gasoline stations, and a dance hall. After the boom ended, workers moved to other fields or to jobs in larger cities, and Penwell's population began to fall steadily.

PEP
Northwest Texas • Hockley County • 35

When land from the Yellow House Ranch went on the market in 1923, some of it was used to found a Catholic colony settled by families of German descent. The colony was originally called Ledwig for its pastor, the Reverend Francis Ledwig. Postal officials rejected this name but did accept Pep, a name meant to indicate the vigor of the community's citizens.

PERRYTON
Panhandle • Ochiltree County • 7,894

Perryton, located eight miles from the Oklahoma state line, identifies itself as the "Wheatheart of the Nation" and as the northernmost county seat in Texas. The town was founded in 1919 as a station on the Panhandle & Santa Fe Railway and named after County Judge George M. Perry, an early settler. It rapidly developed as a shipping point for the region, the nation's top wheat-producing area.

PETROLIA
Oklahoma border • Clay County • 813 • puh-TROHL-yuh

Petrolia, established in 1904 on the Wichita Falls & Oklahoma Railroad, attracted oil speculators from the start. But the biggest developments came in 1907, when natural gas was discovered in the Petrolia oil field, and in 1910, when the field's first big producing oil well blew in. Petrolia was named after a Pennsylvania town also located in an oil-producing area.

PETTY
Northeast Texas • Lamar County • 100

This community was known as Lookout until Texas & Pacific Railway trains began arriving here in the 1870s. Train passengers reportedly became alarmed when a conductor called "Lookout!" So the town adopted the name Dowlin, after a local family, and then in 1886 changed its name to Petty, in honor of landowner J. M. Petty.

PFLUGERVILLE
Central Texas • Travis County • 9,357 • FLOO-ger-vil

Pflugerville was named for a pioneer settler, Henry Pfluger, who brought his large family to Texas from Germany in 1849. Other settlers joined them to establish farms after the Civil War. More than a century later, the town was transformed into a busy Austin suburb, with population increasing by more than 50 percent in the first half of the 1990s alone.

PHARR
Far south Texas • Hidalgo County • 40,936

Around 1910, John C. Kelly established this town in partnership with Henry Pharr, a sugar cane grower from Louisiana for whom Kelly named the town. Henry Pharr's effort to establish a sugar cane industry here in the Rio Grande Valley failed, but Kelly took charge of Pharr's irrigation system and provided water for vegetable and cotton farmers.

PICKTON
Northeast Texas • Hopkins County • 90

A small rural community existed here in the late 1870s. Local historians agree that a committee of two residents chose the name Pick Town around 1880 but disagree on the reason. One source attributes the name to the pickaxes swung by workers building East Line & Red River Railroad tracks through this area. Others say that the committee decided on Pick Town simply because it was asked to "pick" a name. Whoever had the final decision, a railroad official or a postal official, decided that Pickton was a better name than Pick Town.

PIERCE
Southeast Texas • Wharton County • 49

Pierce was named in 1881 for cattleman Abel Head "Shanghai" Pierce when the New York, Texas & Mexico Railway built its tracks across Pierce's vast ranchlands in this county. The colorful rancher constructed a depot at his own expense and sought unsuccessfully to have the town designated as the county seat. Pierce was a company town, with homes constructed for ranch employees, and has never had a population greater than 150.

PILOT POINT
North central Texas • Denton County • 3,080

Pilot Point's name refers to its location on top of a ridge where a grove of oak trees with a single tall cottonwood in the center grew. This landmark was

The grave of rancher Abel Head "Shanghai" Pierce. Courtesy of Ray Miller.

visible from a distance to Indians, early settlers, and other travelers, scouts, or guides. The town of Pilot Point was founded in late 1853 or early 1854.

PIPE CREEK
Southwest Texas • Bandera County • 66

This town developed around a trading post located here in 1872 and was named for a nearby stream, Pipe Creek. According to local lore, the creek got its name after an early settler went back to the creek to retrieve his pipe, despite the fact that he and his companions were being pursued by hostile Indians. He found the pipe that had been left behind and safely eluded the pursuers.

PITTSBURG
Northeast Texas • Camp County • 4,446

William Harrison Pitts came here with his family from Warren County, Georgia, in 1854 and contributed 50 acres of land for a townsite. At first the town spelled its name Pittsburgh, but later the "h" was dropped. Since 1874, Pittsburg has been the Camp County seat.

PLAINVIEW
Northwest Texas • Hale County • 22,213

Edwin Lowden Lowe, living on Z. T. Maxwell's sheep ranch in 1887, suggested the name Plainview for the post office to be opened here. He noted that the site provided a fine, unobstructed view in all directions. The Pecos & Northern Texas Railway arrived in Plainview on the last day of 1906, starting a new era in which the town became a shipping center for farm products and livestock, introduced irrigated farming, and saw its population surge.

PLANO
North central Texas • Collin County • 206,600 • PLAY-noh

Pioneers settled in this area in the 1840s, and William Forman, a farmer from Kentucky, opened a general store in 1851. The town took its name for the area's level terrain: Plano comes from the Spanish word for "plain." Until the 1960s, Plano remained a modest-sized agricultural community. But it then began developing, first as a bustling suburb of Dallas and next as a commercial, financial and technological center, home to the corporate headquarters of Electronic Data Systems, J.C. Penney, and other major companies.

PLEASANTON
South Texas • Atascosa County • 8,691

Pleasanton was founded in 1858 as a new county seat to replace Navatasco, which had been plagued by frequent Indian raids. John Bowen, first postmaster of San Antonio, conceived the idea of establishing this town at the juncture of the Atascosa River and Bonita Creek. He named Pleasanton in honor of his friend John Pleasants, a Pennsylvanian whom Stephen F. Austin induced to settle in Texas. Pleasants served in the Texas revolutionary army and fought at the Battle of San Jacinto. Later in the nineteenth century, Pleasanton was a gathering ground for the cattle drives northward, giving rise to the town's claim to be "Birthplace of the Cowboy."

POINTBLANK
Southeast Texas • San Jacinto County • 514

Residents called this community Pointblank, and the officials who authorized a post office here in 1884 accepted the name. It derived from "Blanc Point," the appellation given to this settlement by Florence Dissiway, a French governess for two well-to-do families here, the Henry Robinsons and the Robert Tod Robinsons. She chose the words to describe the community's open, unobstructed terrain.

POLAR
Northwest Texas • Kent County • 10

About 20 farm families lived in this community in 1906, when its post office was established and named for Polar Singletary, daughter of County Commissioner S. H. Singletary. During the Great Depression, farmers moved away from this area, Polar's school consolidated with the nearby Jayton school district, and the post office closed.

PORT ARTHUR
Southeast Texas • Jefferson County • 58,062

This heavily industrialized town was the site of Aurora, a fishing village, in the 1840s. Half a century later, Port Arthur's founder, Midwest railroad promoter Arthur E. Stillwell, used capital from Eastern financiers and Dutch investors to build the Kansas City, Pittsburg & Gulf line south to this area in 1897. He developed the town, which he named for himself, and as a result of his efforts, Port Arthur became a rail terminus with a nine-mile canal, wide enough for ocean-going ships, providing access to the Gulf of Mexico. Discovery of the Spindletop oil field in 1901 led to the construction of pipelines to carry crude oil to newly built refineries at Port Arthur, which offered shipping facilities for petroleum products. The town has been the birthplace of several celebrities, including sports champion Babe Didricksen Zaharias, painter Robert Rauschenberg, and singer Janis Joplin.

PORT BOLIVAR

Gulf Coast • Galveston County • 1,200 • pohrt BAH-lih-ver

Anglo settlers arrived on the Bolivar Peninsula in the early nineteenth century, and in 1893 a real estate company bought almost 3,000 acres of land for development of a town it named Port Bolivar. Like the peninsula on which it is located, Port Bolivar was named for Simon Bolivar, the soldier-statesman who brought freedom from Spanish rule to six Latin-American republics.

PORT ISABEL

Far south Texas • Cameron County • 5,324

This coastal town, named for Queen Isabella of Spain, who financed the voyages of Columbus, was originally settled in the 1830s. First known as El Fronton de Santa Isabel, it served as a supply base for General Zachary Taylor's army at Brownsville—16 miles southwest—during the Mexican War. It was later known as Brazos Santiago, Isabel, and then Point Isabel, until it incorporated as Port Isabel in 1928.

PORTLAND

Gulf Coast • San Patricio and Nueces counties • 14,220

Three real estate companies teamed up to buy this townsite and sell lots at an auction in 1891; one was the New England Land Company, based in Portland, Maine, for which this town took its name. To transport crowds to the auction, the San Antonio & Aransas Pass Railway ran special trains and a chartered steamer brought prospective buyers from Corpus Christi across the bay. The nationwide financial panic of 1893 brought an end to Portland's incipient boom. Hurricanes in 1916 and 1919 also dealt blows to the town, but growth resumed mid-century. Civic leaders have pointed out that Portland, Texas, is almost exactly equidistant from Portland, Maine, and Portland, Oregon.

Port Lavaca
Gulf Coast • Calhoun County • 12,038 • pohrt lah-VAHK-uh

After Thomas McConnell's home was destroyed during a Comanche attack on Victoria, he bought a tract of land from Isidro Benavides and began to develop a community here in 1842. McConnell, a merchant and Republic of Texas congressman, called the town La Vaca, Spanish for "the cow." In its early days, the town prospered as a shipping point for cattle and cattle by-products. Lavaca became the Calhoun County seat in 1846. But after the rival town of Indianola wrested away the seat of county government six years later, a series of misfortunes began that shrank Lavaca's population from 300 to six dozen residents by 1884. Indianola, with a population of some 5,000, suffered great damage and loss of life in an 1875 hurricane, and then was virtually wiped off the map by another hurricane and an accompanying fire ten years later. The town was abandoned, and Lavaca, which came to be known as Port Lavaca, became the county seat again and began a new period of growth.

Post
Northwest Texas • Garza County • 3,673

Breakfast cereal millionaire C. W. Post founded an experimental model town called Post City here in 1907. The town later became the county seat, shortened its name, and grew into an agribusiness and oil center.

Poteet
South Texas • Atascosa County • 3,732 • poh-TEET

Blacksmith Francis Marion Poteet became this town's first postmaster in 1886. He operated the post office at his shop until the late 1890s when it moved to Henry Mumme's general store. Mumme pioneered the growing of strawberries here. The locally produced crop eventually became large enough that, in 1948, the Rotary Club began an annual festival celebrating Poteet as the "Strawberry Capital of Texas."

Prairie Lea
South central Texas • Caldwell County • 255

General Sam Houston named this town in 1839 while serving in the Congress of the Republic of Texas after his term as president (the constitution barred him from holding a second term). He chose the name for beautiful 20-year-old Margaret Lea of Marion, Alabama, whom he met at a party given by her sister and married in 1840 after a year's courtship.

PRAIRIE VIEW
Southeast Texas • Waller County • 4,170

This location was once the Alta Vista plantation, a name that, like the current one, suggests an extensive open view. After the land became state property in 1876, the legislature used it to establish the historically black college now known as Prairie View A&M University.

PRESIDIO
Far west Texas • Presidio County • 3,558 • pruh-SIH-dih-oh

Spanish explorer Cabeza de Vaca arrived in the early sixteenth century at this location on the Rio Grande, where an Indian village existed, and gave it the name La Junta de las Cruces. Later, other travelers named it San Juan Evangelista and then La Junta de los Rios. By the early nineteenth century it was called Presidio, or "fortress." Two early Anglo settlers built private forts in the area. Population grew after the Kansas City, Mexico & Orient Railway built its tracks here in 1930, and Presidio incorporated.

PURMELA
Central Texas • Coryell County • 61 • per-MEE-luh

Martin Dremien, proprietor of a general store, founded Purmela and became its first postmaster in 1879. Dremien is said to have proposed naming the post office for his sweetheart, Furmela, but postal officials erroneously approved the name as Purmela.

PYOTE
West Texas • Ward County • 371 • PYE-oht

Pyote was founded during a three-day barbecue in 1907 at which townsite lots were sold. The Texas & Pacific Railway built a telegraph station here in 1881 before sending its rail construction crews to this area. Historians offer two explanations for Pyote's odd name: either it was derived from the way Chinese laborers building the railroad pronounced "coyote," or it was a misspelling of peyote, the hallucinatory cactus.

Comanche chief Quanah Parker. Courtesy of Houston Metropolitan Research Center, Houston Public Library.

QUANAH

Oklahoma border • Hardeman County • 3,295 • KWAH-nuh

The Fort Worth & Denver City Railway laid out Quanah's townsite in 1884 and sold town lots the next year. The name honors Quanah Parker, a native Texan and last of the great Comanche chiefs. Two newspapers began publishing in 1890 and merged four years later as the *Quanah Tribune-Chief.*

QUEMADO
Southwest Texas • Maverick County • 426 • kuh-MAH-doh

This town was named for its location in the Quemado (or "burned") Valley, so called by Spanish explorers who theorized the terrain had been affected by ancient volcanic eruptions. The Quemado community consisted of about 100 settlers in 1920, but population increased with the introduction of irrigated farming.

QUITAQUE
Panhandle • Briscoe County • 509 • KIT-uh-kway

Quitaque, a town settled in the early 1890s, was named for Charles Goodnight's Quitaque Ranch. Goodnight had bought vast tracts of Texas Panhandle land a decade earlier, paying 22 cents an acre. He named his ranch for Quitaque Creek, understanding its name to be an Indian word meaning "end of the trail."

RAINBOW
Central Texas • Somervell County • 76

Residents of this rural community in the 1890s decided to apply for a post office. When they gathered to consider possible names to submit, a thunderstorm broke out and a rainbow followed, inspiring their choice.

RAISIN
Gulf Coast • Victoria County • 50

Postal officials rejected several names proposed in 1892 for this town's post office. They finally gave their approval to Raisin, a name suggested after rancher J. K. Reeves showed friends the grapes grown in his new vineyard. The Raisin community has maintained a population of approximately 50 throughout most of its history.

RANGER
Central Texas • Eastland County • 2,911

Ranger, a classic example of the Texas oil boom town, derived its name from the Texas Ranger camp that existed near this location in the 1870s. In 1917, a year when farmers were plagued by drought, drillers struck oil on John McClesky's farm and set off a chaotic, speculative boom that at its height attracted an estimated 30,000 people here. When the boom ended in 1920, most oil field workers and speculators left Ranger—some as millionaires, others on foot.

RAYMONDVILLE
Far south Texas • Willacy County • 9,582

Edward B. Raymond, a former manager of the giant King Ranch's southern division, bought 800 acres of land at this location. On it, he developed a townsite named for himself and began selling lots in 1904. Raymondville's population rose steadily as the town became a commercial center for citrus growers, truck farmers, and agribusiness enterprises.

REALITOS
South Texas • Duval County • 250 • ree-uh-LEE-tus

This community was established in the mid-1880s. Its name is said to derive from small Mexican military camps, called "realitos," that had existed in the vicinity. By 1892, Realitos had 800 residents, a school, and two churches.

RED OAK
Central Texas • Ellis County • 5,000

An abundance of opossums prompted settlers in the 1840s to call this place Possum Trot. In 1849, the community was renamed for Red Oak Creek. It remained largely rural until the middle of the twentieth century, when commuters to Dallas and other Metroplex cities began to move here.

REDWATER
Arkansas border • Bowie County • 872

Redwater originated as a settlement around the Daniels & Spence Sawmill in 1875. The sawmill owners named the town Ingersoll, after the former Illinois state attorney general Robert Green Ingersoll, nationally known as a lecturer espousing agnosticism. Not long after a big revival meeting at Ingersoll resulted in some 110 conversions, church members sought to change the town name. Voters approved Redwater, suggested by the red tint of the town's well water, in an 1894 election.

REFUGIO

Gulf Coast • Refugio County • 3,190 • reh-FYOOR-ih-oh

1795 MISSION NUESTRA SENORA DEL REFUGIO 1995
MISSION STATION
10 TH JANUARY 1995
REFUGIO, TEXAS 78377

This town began in 1834 as a settlement around a Spanish mission, Nuestra Senora del Refugio. It was the site of a battle during the Texas Revolution, and hardships during the Civil War almost turned it into a ghost town. Refugio's population later rebounded, boosted in part by St. Louis, Brownsville & Mexico Railway service that began in 1907 and the discovery of oil in Refugio County in 1928.

REKLAW

East Texas • Cherokee and Rusk counties • 270 • REK-law

When the Texas & New Orleans Railroad extended its tracks through this East Texas area in 1902, land owned by Margaret L. Walker was chosen for a townsite. Citizens wanted to open a post office named Walker in her honor, but postal officials rejected the name, probably to avoid confusion with mail addressed to the post office at Waller, Texas. When the name was resubmitted spelled backward as Reklaw, it won their approval.

RICE

East central Texas • Navarro and Ellis counties • 617

When the Houston & Texas Central Railway built its tracks through this area in 1872, the town of Rice was established. It was named for William Marsh Rice, the wealthy financier and philanthropist who promoted and invested in the rail line, donated land for a church site and cemetery here, and founded Rice University in Houston.

RICHARDSON

North central Texas • Dallas and Collin counties • 86,700

Richardson was founded in 1873 at a site ten miles north of Dallas on the Houston & Texas Central Railroad. When a post office opened in 1874, it was named Richardson—either for E. H. Richardson, the contractor for construction of the railroad's tracks from Dallas to Denton, or A. S. Richardson, a railroad employee. In the 1950s, this farming community began its transformation into "the electronic suburb" now home to dozens of high-tech companies and the University of Texas at Dallas.

RICHMOND
Southeast Texas • Fort Bend County • 13,403

Richmond, the historic seat of Fort Bend County, is named for Virginia's state capital. It was founded in 1837 and incorporated that year under the laws of the Republic of Texas.

RIO GRANDE CITY
Far south Texas • Starr County • 12,224

Rio Grande City originated in 1847 on land from Henry Clay Davis' ranch. Davis used Austin as his model for the town's broad streets. The city is now an international port of entry, connected to the Mexican town of Camargo by a bridge across the river.

RISING STAR
Central Texas • Eastland County • 913

Settler Tom Anderson opened this town's general store and post office in his home in 1880. One historian believes D. D. McConnell of Eastland suggested the name Rising Star, while another relates that settlers argued all night over a name for the town, then "saw the morning star as they started home, and agreed to call it Rising Star."

A group of early settlers gathered at Rising Star. Courtesy of Houston Metropolitan Research Center, Houston Public Library.

RIVIERA
Gulf Coast • Kleberg County • 1,064

Minnesota land promoter Theodore F. Koch founded this town in 1907 after buying a tract of land from Henrietta King of the King Ranch family. Koch chose the name Riviera, saying the site reminded him of the south coast of France. He arranged for a special train to run once or twice a month from Chicago and bring prospective buyers to see the lots available for purchase. By 1910, Riviera had a post office, a school, a hotel, and several stores. The town faced near disaster in 1915 and 1916, first from a harsh drought and next from a devastating hurricane. But newcomers arrived to take the places of those who departed, and Riviera continued to grow.

ROANOKE
North central Texas • Denton County • 1,950

When the Texas & Pacific Railway extended its tracks through Denton County in 1881, a railroad surveyor is said to have named the townsite here for his home town, Roanoke, Virginia. Recorded in an account of a 1548 expedition, Roanoke is believed to be the oldest place name or word adopted from an Indian language into English. According to scholar George Stewart, it is probably Algonquian and has various meanings, such as "northern people," "wampum," and "white shell place."

ROBERT LEE
West central Texas • Coke County • 1,301

Landowners L. B. Harris and R. E. Cartledge founded this town in 1889 and named it for General Robert E. Lee. A decade before the Civil War, Lee had served at Camp Cooper in West Texas.

ROBSTOWN
Gulf Coast • Nueces County • 13,227

A Washington, D.C., real estate developer, George Payl, founded Robstown about 1906, choosing this location because of its railroad junction. He named the town for 35-year-old Robert Driscoll, Jr., who left his New York law practice to manage his family's extensive ranchlands and other property in South Texas.

ROCKDALE
East central Texas • Milam County • 5,720

Mrs. B. F. Ackerman, whose husband donated land for development of a townsite here in 1873, named Rockdale for a 12-foot-high rock near the site. Rockdale incorporated in 1878 and grew rapidly as a shipping and supply center for farmers and stockmen. Its population tripled during the 1950s when a big Alcoa aluminum plant was built here.

ROCKPORT
Gulf Coast • Aransas County • 6,285

Rockport's name derives from a ledge of shellrock that underlies the shore of Aransas Bay. The town became the Aransas County seat in 1872. Meatpacking was a major industry in Rockport and other coastal towns during the cattle boom of the 1870s, but then began to decline with competition from Chicago and Kansas City packing plants. Shipping, shipbuilding, the shrimping industry, and oil drilling have enhanced Rockport's economy.

ROCKWALL
Northeast Texas • Rockwall County • 14,600

In 1854, W. B. Bowles sold Elijah Elgin a 40-acre tract on a hill overlooking the East Fork of the Trinity River. Benjamin Boydstun joined them in developing the land as a townsite. All three agreed upon Rockwall as the town's name. Three years earlier, farmers digging a well discovered a natural geological formation, a subsurface rock wall that crossed underneath the area. In 1873, Rockwall became the seat of Rockwall County, the smallest of the state's 254 counties by area.

ROMA
Far south Texas • Starr County • 10,455

Historians have two theories about the naming of Roma in 1848. A missionary group, the Oblates of Mary Immaculate, which was preparing to establish a mission here, may have suggested the name "because this location has seven hills just as does Rome, the Eternal City of Italy." But Lieutenant W. H. Chatfield wrote that Roma was named for Major Richard Roman of Victoria, who served in the Mexican War and was wounded at the storming of Monterrey.

ROOSEVELT
Southwest Texas • Kimble County • 98

W. B. Waggoner founded this community and named it in honor of Theodore Roosevelt, who is said to have visited the area with the First U.S. Volunteer Cavalry, popularly known as the Rough Riders. Roosevelt's post office opened in 1898 and, as it did then, primarily serves residents of the area's ranches.

ROPESVILLE
Northwest Texas • Hockley County • 507

Jim Jarrott led homesteaders into this area in 1901 after the Spade Ranch made some of its land available for "colonization." The ranch's owner, Isaac Ellwood, also donated land to the South Plains & Santa Fe Railway so that it would build tracks and a depot here. Cowboys from the Spade Ranch constructed rope corrals to hold cattle awaiting rail shipment, and the Santa Fe agreed with their request to name the depot Ropes. A post office opened here in 1920 with the name Ropesville.

ROSEBUD
Central Texas • Falls County • 1,596

The Texas Townsite Company established Rosebud in 1889 at the site of a rural community that had been known at various times as Mormon, Pool's Crossing, and Greer's Horsepen. Postmaster Allen Taylor gave the new town its name. He greatly admired the rose bushes that Mrs. J. L. Mullins brought along when her family settled here. Years ago, the *Rosebud News* launched a still-active project that called for "a rosebud in every yard" and offered cuttings to residents without rosebushes.

ROSENBERG
Southeast Texas • Fort Bend County • 27,444

Rosenberg originated in the heyday of Texas railroad expansion, when the Gulf, Colorado & Santa Fe established a station here in 1880 at its junction with the Galveston, Harrisburg & San Antonio line. From this junction, the New York, Texas & Mexican Railway tracks were extended to Victoria. Within the next decade, an influx of German, Czech, and Polish immigrants helped push Rosenberg's population to 1,000. The town was named in honor of Henry Rosenberg, a Galveston financier, philanthropist, and railroad president.

ROSHARON
Gulf Coast • Brazoria County • 435 • roh-SHEH-r'n

When George W. Collins bought property here about 1900, he named it the Rose of Sharon Garden Ranch. He explained that the wild roses he found reminded him of a rose variety, the Rose of Sharon, in his native England. When Collins succeeded in obtaining a post office in 1912 for this community, the name Rose of Sharon was shortened to Rosharon.

ROSS
Central Texas • McLennan County • 220

Ross, established in the early 1870s as a stop on the Houston & Texas Central Railway, was named for Lawrence Sullivan Ross, sheriff of McLennan County, who earlier served with distinction as a Texas Ranger and a Confederate Army brigadier general. Later, Ross became governor, serving from 1887 to 1891, and then was named president of the Agricultural & Mechanical College of Texas, now Texas A&M University. Sul Ross State University at Alpine was named in his honor.

ROUND ROCK
Central Texas • Williamson County • 50,656

Settlers formed this community in the late 1840s. Thomas C. Oatts, who was appointed postmaster in 1851, and his fishing partner, Jacob Harrell, proposed the town name. They often fished together from a large limestone rock in Brushy Creek, near their homes. The small farming village changed little until the International & Great Northern Railroad built its tracks through Williamson County in 1876, prompting Round Rock citizens to move their community a short distance to the railroad. The town prospered, and was transformed again in recent decades, as housing and commercial development spilled over from metropolitan Austin. Most notably, Round Rock is home to Dell Computer Corporation's corporate headquarters.

ROUND TOP
Central Texas • Fayette County • 91

One of the smallest incorporated towns in Texas, Round Top traces the history of its one-square-mile site to 1831. The community was first known as the Townsend Settlement after a family of early settlers. Alwin H. Soergel, an author and musician, moved here and in 1847 built a white house with an octagonal tower. The tower, viewed at a distance, appeared to be round and gave the town its name.

ROUNDUP
Northwest Texas • Hockley County • 20

W. H. Simpson, a Santa Fe Railway official, is said to have chosen the ranch-style name of Roundup. The community developed on land that was originally part of the famed Spade Ranch, after the Santa Fe established a rail switch here in 1912 and made it a shipping point for ranch and farm products. Roundup had a cotton gin and a grain elevator in the 1940s, along with about 50 residents.

ROWLETT
North central Texas • Dallas and Rockwall counties • 38,700

Rowlett was founded on the Missouri-Kansas-Texas Railroad, which reached this area in 1886. The town was named for Rowlett Creek, which in turn was named for Daniel Rowlett, owner of the Collin County property through which the creek flowed on its way downstream to Dallas County. A pioneer surveyor and physician, Rowlett served as quartermaster in General Sam Houston's revolutionary army and was granted the Collin County property for his military service. After Texas won its independence, Rowlett became a legislator and civic leader.

ROYALTY
West Texas • Ward County • 196

The Shipley Hazlett No. 1 became Ward County's first producing oil well in 1928, and this community formed to provide services to the Shipley field and its workers. It was known briefly as Allentown, for a local landowner, then renamed Royalty when its post office opened in 1929. Oil companies paid landowners a percentage of income—a royalty— from producing wells.

Rusk

East Texas • Cherokee County • 4,576

In 1846 the Texas Legislature established Rusk and designated it the Cherokee County seat. The town was named for Thomas Jefferson Rusk of Nacogdoches, who was a major general in the Texas militia, served as chief justice of the Texas republic's supreme court, and was elected to the U.S. Senate when Texas became a state.

Sacul

East Texas • Nacogdoches County • 170 • SA-k'l

When the Texas & New Orleans Railroad extended its tracks to this area in 1901, the town of Sacul developed on land once owned by the Lucas family. Postal officials rejected the name Lucas for the town's post office, but accepted Sacul, the Lucas name spelled backward.

Saint Hedwig

South Texas • Bexar County • 1,799

Immigrants from Silesia in central Europe founded this town in the mid-1850s. They constructed the town's first church out of logs, later replacing it with a stone building. A post office opened in 1860 with the name Cottage Hill. In 1877 it was renamed Saint Hedwig, for the Silesian patron saint.

Saint Jo

Oklahoma border • Montague County • 1,134

Irb Boggess and Joseph Howell bought some land here in 1872 to develop as a townsite. Boggess, owner of the Stonewall Saloon, named the townsite Joe for his friend Howell. The name changed to Saint Jo, reportedly after Boggess jocularly declared Howell's opposition to the sale of liquor in town "saintly."

San Angelo

West central Texas • Tom Green County • 90,005

After Fort Concho was built nearby in 1867, Bart J. DeWitt established a trading post here. Santa Angela, the town that sprang up around DeWitt's store, was chosen in 1882 as the Tom Green County seat. There are several stories about the origin of San Angelo's name. One holds that DeWitt named the town Santa Angela in memory of his late wife, Caroline Angela. In another version, DeWitt chose the name for his sister-in-law Angelina, a San Antonio nun. According to each of these stories, postal officials changed the name to San Angelo. By the 1920s, San Angelo was an oil and gas trade center and headquarters for the Texas wool industry.

1836 - 1996

MAR 6 1996

160th Anniversary
Alamo Station
San Antonio, TX 78205

The Alamo

SAN ANTONIO
South Texas • Bexar County • 1,114,579

Domingo Teran de los Rios, governor of Coahuila and Texas, named the San Antonio River after happening upon it during the feast day of St. Anthony of Padua in 1691. An early-eighteenth-century settlement adjacent to the river took San Antonio as its name. A century later, Texas rebels fought here against Mexican troops in the siege of Bexar and the Battle of the Alamo. The 1860 census showed that San Antonio had passed Galveston as the largest city in the state. Growth continued as five railroads arrived and business activity expanded. A wave of immigrants from Mexico reached San Antonio after 1910, making cultural and economic contributions just as earlier waves of settlers from Germany and the U.S. South had done. Famous San Antonio natives include Joan Crawford and comedienne Carol Burnett.

SAN AUGUSTINE
East Texas • San Augustine County • 2,375 • san AW-g's-teen

Ayish Indians and Spaniards inhabited this locale until the 1790s, when small numbers of Anglo pioneers from the Old South began arriving and settling here. In 1833, Thomas McFarland surveyed and laid out 356 town lots for a permanent settlement. Mexican officials named the town San Augustine in honor of the fourth-century Christian philosopher. Just a few years later, San Augustine sent delegates to sign the Texas Declaration of Independence.

SAN BENITO
Far south Texas • Cameron County • 23,940 • san buh-NEE-tuh

Ranch hand Rafael Morena is said to have suggested the name of this town as a tribute to his employer, Benjamin Hicks, a man he admired and who was known to his workers as "Don Benito." Hicks was a partner in the San Benito Land & Water Company, which subdivided town lots and put them up for sale in 1907.

SAN DIEGO
South Texas • Duval County • 5,137

Herdsmen working for rancher Julian Flores around 1815 are believed to have been this area's first settlers. In 1819, Flores and his family gave instructions for the founding of a town on San Diego Creek. It was known first as Perezville for Pablo Perez, who built some stone houses at the site and brought families to live in them. However, when a post office opened, the name changed to San Diego after the creek. In the 1860s and 1870s, the town and its surrounding ranches thrived while wool prices were high, and San Diego became the Duval County seat. During the next 50 years, the town gained importance as an agricultural and commercial center—but at the same time earned a reputation for gunfights and slayings, the violence often stemming from disputes between political enemies.

SAN ELIZARIO
Far west Texas • El Paso County • 4,794 • san el-ih-ZAH-rih-oh

Spain established a military garrison called Presidio of San Elizario here near the Rio Grande in 1789. The settlement that grew up around the presidio was named San Elizario. After Mexico won its independence from Spain, San Elizario was part of the state of Chihuahua. When the Treaty of Guadalupe Hidalgo was signed in 1848, it became part of Texas.

San Felipe
Southeast Texas • Austin County • 849 • san fuh-LEEP

In 1823 Stephen F. Austin planned a town at this location to serve as the unofficial capital of his colony. Luciano Garcia, Mexico's governor of Texas, was friendly to Austin's colony and proposed naming the town San Felipe de Austin to honor both Austin and the patron saint of Felipe de la Garza, the governor of Mexico's eastern interior provinces. The town played a significant role in nineteenth-century Texas history as many early colonists and, later, freed slaves and immigrants came here, some to stay, most to stop temporarily before moving on to points eleswhere in Texas.

Sanger
North central Texas • Denton County • 4,319

The Gulf, Colorado & Santa Fe Railway founded this farming and live-stock town in 1886 and named it for the Sanger family, pioneer Texas retailers who shipped and received merchandise via the railway. Sanger's post office was established at F. M. Ready's home, which also became a hotel and eating place.

San Juan
Far south Texas • Hidalgo County • 21,147 • san WAHN

San Juan was named for John Closner, who sold 406 acres of land in 1910 to the San Juan Townsite Company. Closner, a former stagecoach driver and Hidalgo County sheriff, became a major landowner, farmer, and political leader in the Rio Grande Valley. The townsite company developed a community on Closner's land that grew steadily into a farm-ing and commercial center. By 1925, businesses included a cotton gin, a cotton compress, and a cannery.

San Marcos
South central Texas • Hays County • 35,979

San Marcos is named for the San Marcos River, which flows from springs within the town. The Spanish governor of Texas sought unsuc-cessfully in 1808 to establish a town called San Marcos de Neve here, but repeated Indian attacks and a flood thwarted the effort. Settler William W. Moon arrived around 1845, and other pioneers soon joined him to form a lasting settlement.

SANTA ANNA

Central Texas • Coleman County • 1,241

Settlers began arriving in this area in the 1870s, a community took form in the early 1880s, and the town of Santa Anna began growing rapidly in the mid-1880s. It took its name for the Santa Anna Mountains, twin peaks north of the town that had been named for the Penateka Comanche tribal leader, Chief Santa Anna.

An old rock house at the base of Santa Anna Peak. Courtesy of Ray Miller.

SANTA ELENA

Far south Texas • Starr County • 64 • san-tuh LEE-nuh

Santa Elena originated as a small community with a few dozen residents in the 1890s, and throughout the twentieth century its population fluctuated between 15 and 200. Records do not indicate whether the post office was named for a religious saint or for Santa Elena Canyon on the Rio Grande in West Texas. Texas author Jack Maguire reported in 1973 that he found the Santa Elena post office in another town. When Santa Elena's postmaster married, she moved to her husband's home four miles away in La Gloria and had the post office building moved with her. Maguire added: "That's why the highway signs tell the traveler he's in La Gloria, but the sign on the only federal building in town reads 'U.S. Post Office, Santa Elena, Texas.'"

SANTO
North central Texas • Palo Pinto County • 445

J. D. T. Bearden founded a settlement here in the 1850s called Grand Ranch. In the 1870s, the name was changed to Calgando. In the 1880s, it was changed again, this time to Cresco, a Latin word meaning "I grow." The next name was Sparta, but postal officials rejected it because there was already a Sparta post office in Texas. Santo was the replacement name. Historians are unsure whether it was chosen to honor a pioneer resident, John Adam Santo, or a railroad telegrapher, John Santo Stati.

SAN YGNACIO
Far south Texas • Zapata County • 1,200 • san ig-NAH-sih-oh

San Ygnacio, the oldest town in this county, was settled in 1830 by former residents of Revilla, a town on the south side of the Rio Grande. Jesus Trevino, who led the settlers, built a sandstone home that became known as Fort Trevino. The new town was named for St. Ignatius of Loyola, a native of Spain and founder of the Jesuit order. In 1951 residents successfully protested orders to abandon their town to make way for the Falcon Dam.

SARATOGA
Southeast Texas • Hardin County • 1,000

Its earliest settlers named this place New Sour Lake. That name was jettisoned in the 1880s when P. S. Watts began publicizing and promoting a spring of flowing water discovered here, claiming it had restorative powers for those ill or in poor health. He constructed a hotel, cabins, and campsites for visitors attracted by his advertising. The town was renamed Saratoga, for Saratoga Springs, the New York health resort and race track locale. In 1901 J. F. Cotton, who found the medicinal well, discovered another underground resource—oil.

SCHERTZ
South central Texas • Guadalupe, Comal, and Bexar counties • 14,014

In the 1840s, settlers moved here and formed a community they called Cibola Pit. When a post office opened in 1884, it was named Cut Off, for a recent flood that cut off this town from neighboring communities. The present name was adopted in 1899, honoring the Schertz family, pioneer residents who donated land for the depot of the Galveston, Harrisburg & San Antonio Railway in 1875, as well as land for a school site. The family also established the town's first cotton gin, and Sebastian Schertz opened a general store. The last half of the twentieth century transformed Schertz from a farming community into a busy San Antonio suburb bordering Randolph Air Force Base.

SCOTLAND
North central Texas • Archer and Clay counties • 557

This town was founded by a Canadian, settled by Germans, and named Scotland. John H. Meurer moved here in 1907 to develop a tract of land owned by Henry J. Scott of Toronto. Meurer sold town lots to German immigrants recruited from Galveston and other points in Texas. The townsite, named Scotland after Scott, adjoined the newly built Southwestern Railway line. The first train arrived in mid-1908, and farmers soon began shipping cotton and grain to markets.

SEABROOK
Southeast Texas • Harris, Chambers, and Galveston counties • 8,498

Real estate developer John Sydnor founded this town in 1900 and named it for Seabrook Sydnor, his son. Seabrook remained a small town until mid-century, when industrial development in the coastal area caused its population to surge.

SEAGOVILLE
North central Texas • Dallas County • 10,350

T. K. Seago established a general store here in 1876. The farming community that developed around the store was known as Seago for more than three decades. In 1910, the name was changed to Seagoville to avoid confusion with the post office at Segno in Polk County.

SEALY
Southeast Texas • Austin County • 5,529

The Gulf, Colorado & Santa Fe established a railroad yard and roundhouse here in the late 1870s. In 1880, when a post office opened, it was named for George Sealy, a Galveston banker and influential member of

Santa Fe's board of directors. A Brazos River flood in 1899 and the Galveston hurricane of 1900 violently disrupted, but did not end, Sealy's progress. Among the businesses that have helped build the town's economy is the now nationally known Sealy Mattress Company.

SEGUIN
South central Texas • Guadalupe County • 21,941 • seh-GEEN

Members of Matthew Caldwell's Gonzales Rangers founded this community in 1838 as Walnut Springs. A year later, the name was changed to Seguin in honor of Juan Nepomuceno Seguin, who served in Sam Houston's revolutionary army. It was Seguin who provided a proper military burial for those who died defending the Alamo. He later served as a senator of the Republic of Texas and as mayor of San Antonio. The town of Seguin has prospered from diversified agriculture, including peach orchards, Christmas tree farms, and pecans that are shipped nationwide.

SEMINOLE
New Mexico border • Gaines County • 6,765

Seminole was founded and designated as the Gaines County seat in 1905. The town name likely came from Seminole Draw, which rises in western Gaines County and runs southeast for 60 miles. Indian Wells, a camping place for Seminole scouts, who found water wells there, was located on the draw. Seminole has been the birthplace of two country music stars: Larry Gatlin, who with his Olney-born siblings formed the Gatlin Brothers; and Tanya Tucker.

SHAMROCK
Panhandle • Wheeler County • 2,106

George Nickel, a sheep rancher who emigrated from Ireland, applied for permission to open a post office here in 1890. He proposed Shamrock as the name, pointing out that a shamrock symbolizes good luck and courage.

SHERMAN
Oklahoma border • Grayson County • 33,528

Sherman was established as the Grayson County seat in 1846. Its name honors a hero of the Texas Revolution, Sidney Sherman, to whom the battle cry "Remember the Alamo" has been credited. During an eventful military and civilian career, Sherman founded the pioneering Buffalo Bayou, Brazos & Colorado Railway, which operated an 83-mile line in southeast Texas.

SHINER
South Texas • Lavaca County • 2,351

Around 1885, landowner Henry B. Shiner gave the San Antonio & Aransas Pass Railway 250 acres for use as a right-of-way and a depot site. The town of Shiner grew up around the depot and developed into a trade center for Czech and German farmers. Two of the town's enterprises have gained national renown—the Kasper Wire Works, maker of newspaper display racks and other metal products; and the Spoetzl brewery, which produces Shiner Bock and other beers.

SIERRA BLANCA
Far west Texas • Hudspeth County • 700 • see-ehr-a BLANG-kuh

The highest point in the Sierra Blanca mountains is Sierra Blanca Peak, at 6,891 feet above sea level. This town named for the mountain peak had an appropriately lofty beginning in late 1881. Here two railroads met to form a transcontinental link for only the second time in U.S. history. Rail tycoon Jay Gould drove a silver spike to join the Texas & Pacific and Southern Pacific lines, ending the race between construction crews starting from the east and west coasts.

SILVERTON
Panhandle • Briscoe County • 816

Tom Braidfoot became the first settler in this area in 1890 and, joined by several friends, founded a townsite company in early 1891. His wife is said to have suggested Silverton's name because of the silvery reflections of light on the vicinity's many lakes. Silverton defeated two rival townsites, Tarlton and Linguist, to become the Briscoe County seat, and by the early 1900s it developed into a commercial center for the area's ranchers and farmers.

SISTERDALE
South central Texas • Kendall County • 63

Nicolaus Zink, an eccentric Bavarian engineer, founded Sisterdale in 1847 at this location near the Sister Creeks. Over the next four years, Zink was joined by members of the Forty-Eighters, a group of prominent German freethinkers—educational, cultural, and political leaders—who fled Europe after the aborted revolutionary movement of 1848. A farming community, Sisterdale reached its peak population of about 150 in the 1880s.

SLATON
Northwest Texas • Lubbock County • 6,179 • SLAYT-'n

The Santa Fe railroad founded the town of Slaton in 1910 to serve as headquarters for the company's largest operating division. Railroad officials named the town for rancher and banker O. L. Slaton, who made plans to open a bank here. Santa Fe employees and their families moved to Slaton from other locations to be among the earliest residents. The railroad company provided locomotion for Slaton's growth for more than a half century.

SNYDER
West Texas • Scurry County • 12,019

Snyder was named for William Henry "Pete" Snyder, who arrived here in 1878 and built a trading post that developed into a colony of buffalo hunters and traders. The pioneer merchant-trader drew up plans for a townsite in 1882, and two years later his new town was picked as the Scurry County seat. Discovery of the Canyon Reef Oil Field in 1948 produced a boom that temporarily quadrupled Snyder's population, then ended in late 1951.

SONORA
Southwest Texas • Sutton County • 3,069 • suh-NOH-ruh

Sonora, the Sutton County seat, began in the late 1880s, as a settlement around Charles G. Adams' trading post on the Old San Antonio-El Paso Road and around the water well Adams dug nearby. Mrs. Adams named the town for a long-time family employee whose nickname, Sonora, was taken from his home state in Mexico.

SOUR LAKE
Southeast Texas • Hardin County • 1,746

Sour Lake's first settler, Stephen Jackson, arrived in 1835 and camped by one of the springs flowing into the lake that gave this town its name. He found that the mineralized water had a sour taste. For about four decades, beginning around 1850, Sour Lake Springs flourished as a mineral bath and health treatment resort. Two hotels, bath houses, and other facilities were built to accommodate the town's visitors, and entrepreneurs bottled and sold the spring water. After tourism declined, Sour Lake regained its economic health explosively in 1902, when a well drilled here by Great Western Oil Company became a gusher. The surrounding oil field yielded nearly 9,000,000 barrels of oil in 1903, and the boom lured somewhere between 5,000 and 10,000 oil field workers and speculators. The Texas Company, which later became Texaco, got its start at the Sour Lake field. But the exciting boom days soon came to an end and Sour Lake's dozens of saloons closed up.

Sour Lake in the nineteenth century. Courtesy of Ray D. Edmondson.

SPLENDORA

Southeast Texas • Montgomery County • 1,026

Settled in the late 1800s, this town was first called Cox's Switch in honor of Charles Cox, the local stationmaster and switchman for the Houston, East & West Texas Railway. M. S. King applied for a post office in 1896, and, at Cox's request, proposed a new name for the town. His suggestion was Splendora, for "the splendor of the floral environment."

SPRING

Southeast Texas • Harris County • 38,825

Spring was named for Spring Creek, where a trading post was established about 1830 and a surrounding settlement grew up. German immigrants came here in the mid-1840s and began farming, joined during the next quarter century by families from Louisiana and other southern states. During the latter nineteenth and early twentieth century, Spring was a hub of railroad activity as the location of a roundhouse and major switchyards. Population dropped after the railroad operations moved to Houston in 1923, then rose again as Houston's metropolitan growth spread northward.

SPUR

Northwest Texas • Dickens County • 1,131

This town was officially established on the first day of November 1909, when the first Stamford & Northwestern Railroad train reached Spur's depot. W. S. Campbell's combination mortuary and furniture store, the first local business enterprise, opened ten days later. The town developed on land subdivided from the famed Spur Ranch.

STAFFORD

Southeast Texas • Fort Bend and Harris counties • 13,900

The town of Stafford's Point, founded in 1853 as a stop on the Buffalo Bayou, Brazos & Colorado Railway, was named for William Stafford, one of Stephen F. Austin's colonists. Years before the railroad was built, Stafford lived here with his family on a plantation equipped with a horse-powered cotton gin and a cane mill. Families settling near the plantation called the area Stafford's Point, and a post office opened in 1854 with that name. In early 1869 its name changed to Staffordville, then was shortened to Stafford.

STANTON
West Texas • Martin County • 2,519

Stanton was named in 1890 for Abraham Lincoln's secretary of war, Edward McMasters Stanton, who also served as a U.S. Supreme Court justice. Previously, this town was called Marienfeld—"field of Mary"— by its German Catholic settlers. The settlers were recruited by a Kansan, John Jacob Konz, whose goal was to establish a Catholic colony in West Texas. He chose a location on the Texas & Pacific Railway in 1881. Two priests of the Carmelite order traveled to Germany to publicize the colony. The first Catholic church in West Texas was built here.

STEPHENVILLE
North central Texas • Erath County • 15,478

John M. Stephen and his brother, William, were among 30 pioneer settlers who came to this area in 1854. When the Texas Legislature made plans to create Erath County, John Stephen announced that he would donate land for a townsite and a courthouse if the legislature would name the town Stephenville and make it the county seat. The state accepted his offer, and John Stephen later became Stephenville's first postmaster.

STONEWALL
Central Texas • Gillespie County • 245

Israel P. Nunez, who began operating a stagecoach station in this vicinity around 1870, successfully applied for a post office in 1875. It was named Stonewall, for Confederate General Thomas "Stonewall" Jackson. Settlers raised cattle and sheep and established orchards, and the town evolved into a center of peach production. In 1908 future president Lyndon B. Johnson was born in Stonewall.

STRATFORD
Panhandle • Sherman County • 1,913

Stratford is located on land that was owned by Aaron Norton when this area was settled in the mid-1880s. Walter Colton, manager of Norton's properties, laid out the townsite. Historians disagree about Colton's background and why he chose Stratford as the townsite's name. Some say Colton was a Kentuckian who admired Robert E. Lee and

181

named the town for Stratford, Virginia, where Lee was born. Others contend that Colton was an Englishman and named the townsite for Stratford-on-Avon.

STUDY BUTTE
Southwest Texas • Brewster County • 120 • styoo-dih BYOOT

Study Butte originated as a mining town after mercury deposits were discovered here around 1900. It was named for Will Study, first manager of the Big Bend Cinnabar Mine. Profits from the mine gradually diminished and it closed in the early 1940s. Study Butte's economy has since chiefly relied upon visitors to adjacent Big Bend National Park and other tourists.

SUDAN
Northwest Texas • Lamb County • 970

Sudan developed during World War I on land that was previously part of the 77 Ranch owned by Wilson Furneaux and S. J. Wilson. The first postmaster, P. F. Boesen, reportedly suggested the name Sudan because of the suitability of this area's soil for Sudan grass, which is usually grown for hay.

SUGAR LAND
Southeast Texas • Fort Bend County • 54,633

Sugar cane was grown on the Oakland Plantation here in the early nineteenth century. The town of Sugar Land originated in the 1890s after E. H. Cunningham of San Antonio accumulated thousands of acres of land and then proceeded to invest an estimated $1 million in building a sugar refinery and raw sugar mill. Isaac H. Kempner and W. T. Eldredge later bought and updated Cunningham's properties. Kempner created the Imperial Sugar Company, which processed sugar cane grown in Fort Bend County until 1928 and thereafter imported raw sugar for the refinery. In recent decades Sugar Land has become a fast-growing Houston suburb. The 1990 census figure of 24,549 doubled before 1996.

SULPHUR SPRINGS
Northeast Texas • Hopkins County • 14,977

This town originated with the name Bright Star around 1850 and later became the Hopkins County seat. The name was changed to Sulphur

Springs in 1871 as part of an effort to promote the area's healthful mineral springs. Later, the town developed rapidly as a center for farming, dairying, and light manufacturing.

SUNDOWN
Northwest Texas • Hockley County • 1,755

Sundown, a small town founded in 1928, gained widespread publicity when a 1937 oil strike created quick and dramatic growth. News media hailed the community as "Boomtown USA." The town originated on land from the Slaughter Ranch and was named by R. L. "Bob" Slaughter, who said the word "sundown" was in the title of a motion picture he liked. Another story has it that after settlers had engaged in a day-long debate over the town name, one spoke up and said, "Aw, let's just name it Sundown—it's sundown now."

SUNSET
Oklahoma border • Montague County • 300

Early settlers here included Sam Smith, who established a grocery store and, in 1880, applied for permission to open a post office named Smithville. Postal officials rejected that name, since there was an existing Smithville post office in Bastrop County. Instead they substituted Sunset, "since you're so far toward the setting sun."

SWEET HOME
South Texas • Lavaca County • 360

Early settlers found beneficial living conditions here and named their community Sweet Home. A post office opened in 1852, and George West built a hotel, stables, and a general store in 1860. The early 1870s brought Czech, German, and Bohemian immigrants to the town. Sweet Home relocated five miles southward in 1887 to the San Antonio & Aransas Pass rail line.

SWEETWATER
West central Texas • Nolan County • 11,874

Sweetwater was founded in 1881 when Nolan County formed, and the town—which at the time had no permanent buildings—was designated the county seat. In the same year, the Texas & Pacific Railway began operating trains through the town. Both events gave impetus to Sweetwater's initial development, and it soon had a temporary courthouse along with five saloons. The town's name derives from Sweetwater Creek, said to have been named by Texas Rangers who, as they followed Indians across open country, liked the taste of this stream's water better than the bitter-tasting water they found in other creeks.

TAFT
Gulf Coast • San Patricio County • 3,812

Joseph Green, who chose this town's name, was general manager of the Coleman-Fulton Pasture Company and its vast landholdings. Charles Taft was a major investor in the company and the half brother of William Howard Taft, U.S. president from 1909 to 1913. Green decided in 1904 to build a new town called Taft on the Coleman-Fulton ranchlands, to replace the small settlement, Mesquital, that had existed at a railroad flag stop there since 1886. The Coleman-Fulton ranch also took the name Taft. It was visited by President Taft, who stayed for four days at the Taft Ranch headquarters, La Quinta, a three-story mansion on Corpus Christi Bay. Coleman-Fulton divested its properties at a public auction in 1921. No longer a company town, Taft incorporated eight years later.

TALCO
Northeast Texas • Franklin County • 613

A community called Goolesboro had existed near here since 1878. But because one or more other post offices in Texas had similar names, this town and its post office changed names in 1910. Talco, the new name submitted to postal officials, came from the initials printed on the wrapper of a candy bar distributed by the Texas, Arkansas & Louisiana Candy Company. Oil was discovered in this vicinity in 1936, and Talco's population zoomed to 5,000 while the boom lasted. Because the low-gravity oil produced here was ideal for making asphalt, Talco soon heralded itself as the world's asphalt capital.

TARZAN
West Texas • Martin County • 80

Tarzan, the hero of Edgar Rice Burroughs' adventure novels, was one of the 14 names for this town's post office that storekeeper Tant Lindsey suggested to Washington postal officials in the mid-1920s. Officials granted the request for a post office, appointed Lindsey postmaster, and chose the name Tarzan.

TAYLOR
Central Texas • Williamson County • 14,711

This town, originally named Taylorsville, was established in 1876 and named in honor of Edward M. Taylor, an official of the Houston Belt & Terminal Railroad. The Texas Land Company auctioned off lots so successfully that there were 1,000 residents in 1878. The name Taylorsville was shortened to Taylor in 1892.

TELEGRAPH
Southwest Texas • Kimble County • 3

In 1900, a post office called Telegraph opened to serve this picturesque ranching area. It was named for nearby Telegraph Canyon, where trees were cut for use as telegraph poles in the late 1870s, when the U.S. Army was extending telegraph lines to its West Texas forts. Telegraph's population has never exceeded double digits.

TELEPHONE
Oklahoma border • Fannin County • 210

Postal officials rejected several names Pete Hindman proposed when he applied to open a post office here in 1885. Hindman, the proprietor of this community's general store, next suggested the name Telephone. He pointed out that the area's only telephone was located in his store.

TELFERNER
Gulf Coast • Victoria County • 700 • TELF-ner

Telferner originated as a station on the New York, Texas & Mexican Railway in 1882. It was named for Count Joseph Telfener but was erroneously spelled with an extra "r." Telfener, a native of Naples, was born Giuseppe Telfener but adopted the first name Joseph when he came to the United States. King Victor Emmanuel II of Italy gave him the title of count in recognition of his engineering achievements. With experience as a financier and contractor for railroads in South America, Telfener became president of the New York, Texas & Mexican Railway Company, chartered in 1880. He brought 1,200 Italian workers to South Texas to build the railroad, which became known locally as the "Macaroni Line." But the project was abandoned by the end of 1882, with only 91 of the planned 350 miles of track completed.

TELL
Panhandle • Childress County • 63

After this village was founded in 1887, a post office named Lee opened, then closed in 1893. During this time, the community earned the nickname Tattle-Tale Flats, from the propensity of certain residents to testify voluntarily before county grand juries. The post office reopened in 1895, with its name changed to Tell, an abridged version of the town's tattling nickname.

TEMPLE
Central Texas • Bell County • 50,419

Temple was founded in 1880 and named for a Civil War veteran, Bernard M. Temple, who was chief engineer for the Gulf, Colorado &

Temple's Railroad and Pioneer Museum, located in a former depot. Courtesy of Ray Miller.

Santa Fe Railway. The railway established a townsite here, sold 157 business lots and 28 residential lots at a public auction, and made the new town its division headquarters.

TENNESSEE COLONY
East Texas • Anderson County • 300

Arriving in 1847 by wagon train, settlers from Tennessee founded a community here and called it Tennessee Colony as a salute to their home state. The new residents established several cotton plantations and built a log schoolhouse.

TENNYSON
West central Texas • Coke County • 35

Sam C. Sayner, a native of England who settled here around 1880, named this tiny village for Alfred, Lord Tennyson, the English poet. Tennyson reached its maximum population, around 50 residents, in the 1940s.

TERLINGUA
Southwest Texas • Brewster County • 25 • ter-LING-gwuh

Terlingua flourished as a mining town in the first three decades of the twentieth century, after quicksilver, or mercury, deposits were discovered here. A post office opened in 1899 with the name Terlingua, a corruption of *tres lenguas,* meaning "three languages" or "three tongues." Historians have differed as to whether the reference is to the three forks of Terlingua Creek or to three Indian languages. Mining operations closed down in the 1940s, and Terlingua became a ghost town. It was revived by Big Bend area tourism and international publicity about the annual world championship chili cook-offs that began around 1970.

TERRELL
Northeast Texas • Kaufman County • 13,050

John G. Nash and C. C. Moore bought 320 acres here in 1873 and laid out a townsite on the route of the Texas & Pacific rail line being constructed across East Texas to Dallas. As new residents arrived, the town gained a post office, which was named for early settler Robert A. Terrell. The North Texas Insane Asylum, later renamed Terrell State Hospital, opened here in 1885.

TEXARKANA

Arkansas border • Bowie County • 33,252 (Texas side)

This town straddles the Texas-Arkansas state line at a spot 20 miles from the Louisiana border. Its name, which combines the first syllable of Texas, the first syllable of Arkansas, and the last two syllables of Louisiana, was coined at an unknown date. Settlers here were using it even before the Texas & Pacific Railway established a townsite for the Texas side of the city in 1873.

TEXON

West Texas • Reagan County • 12

Levi Smith, president of the Big Lake Oil Company, founded Texon in 1924 to provide housing for his employees and their families. He named the town for the Texon Oil & Land Company. Months earlier, the company had drilled the Santa Rita discovery well that opened up the Big Lake pool and led to the development of West Texas's Permian Basin as a major center of oil and gas production.

THORNDALE

East central Texas • Milam County • 1,333

In 1878, soon after the rail line had finished building its tracks here, an employee of the International & Great Northern Railroad gave this town its name, noting that the area had a plentiful supply of prickly pear cactus and other thorny plants.

THRIFTY

Central Texas • Brown County • 25

By the end of the Civil War, a sizeable settlement had grown up around the I C Ranch headquarters here. A post office opened in 1875, named Jim Ned for nearby Jim Ned Creek. In 1880 the post office was renamed Thrifty, apparently in tribute to the industrious and frugal character of the community's residents.

TILDEN

South Texas • McMullen County • 450

Pioneers settling here at the mouth of the Frio River in 1858 called their settlement Rio Frio and saw it grow enough to add a general store and a saloon in 1862. By the mid-1860s, this village became known as Dog Town because ranchers in the area used packs of dogs to round up their cattle. Although a townsite was established with the name Colfax, Dog Town was the name of the post office that opened in 1871. Dog Town became the McMullen County seat in 1877, but its name was changed to Tilden, for Samuel J. Tilden, who lost the 1876 presidential election to Rutherford B. Hayes by one electoral vote.

TIN TOP
North central Texas • Parker County • 12

Tin Top's name came from the galvanized metal roof of the cotton gin built here in 1909. Gleaming in the sunlight, the roof was visible from miles away. The name Tin Top was then given to the suspension bridge that Parker County erected here in 1906 across the Brazos River. In 1982 the bridge was destroyed during a winter storm.

TOKIO
Northwest Texas • Terry County • 60

Mrs. H. D. Ware, mother of the town's first postmaster, is said to have named Tokio for Tokyo, the capital of Japan. Mrs. Ware said she had no reason for the choice other than the fact that she liked the name.

TOMBALL
Southeast Texas • Harris County • 7,208

Tomball originated in 1906 as a railroad stop called Peck on the northern edge of Harris County, where the Trinity & Brazos Valley Railroad built a freight terminal and shipping pens for livestock. In 1907 Peck was renamed Tomball, in honor of Thomas Henry Ball, a prominent Houston lawyer and former congressman. The farming town turned into a boom town in 1933 when drillers struck oil here. In 1935, Humble Oil signed a contract with municipal officials to provide free natural gas and water to Tomball residents for 90 years in exchange for drilling rights within the city limits. Robert Ripley's "Believe It or Not" syndicated feature told newspaper readers that Tomball was the only city with free natural gas, free water, and no cemetery.

Topsey

Central Texas • Coryell County • 20

Topsey, a rural community settled around 1900, has ranged in population between 20 and 100 ever since. Its post office, which operated from 1901 until 1918, was named Topsey for a resident's favorite mule. The name of the mule's owner went unrecorded.

Trent

Central Texas • Taylor County • 323

The Texas & Pacific Railway, establishing stations in 1881 on its new rail line westward from Abilene, planned to name this place Eskota and the next station Trent. But signboards for the stations were erroneously switched. The rail station here became known as Trent, named for pioneer settler I. R. Trent—who continued to live in the place that was named Eskota instead of Trent.

Tuleta

South Texas • Bee County • 110 • too-LEE-tuh

Tuleta originated as a Mennonite colony founded in 1906 by Peter Unzicker, a German Mennonite minister, who brought the colonists from Cullom, Illinois. Unzicker bought the 54-acre townsite from the Chittum-Miller Ranch and named it for rancher J. M. Chittum's daughter.

Tulia

Panhandle • Swisher County • 5,304 • TOOL-yuh

Founders of this town intended to name it Tule after nearby Tule Creek. However, a clerical error on their post office application rendered the name as Tulia, and so a postal office by that name opened in 1887.

Tyler

Northeast Texas • Smith County • 82,078

The Texas Legislature established this town in 1846 as the seat of newly created Smith County, naming it in honor of President John Tyler for his support of Texas statehood. Tyler became a flourishing business center, and local agriculture included large-scale commercial production of rosebushes. The town also became a regional base for the oil and gas industry.

UNCERTAIN
Northeast Texas • Harrison County • 221

The town of Uncertain consists mainly of fishing camps, lakeside dwellings, restaurants, and liquor stores. It lies on the shores of Caddo Lake, a body of water that spans the Texas-Louisiana state line. Uncertain's name comes from a nearby point, Uncertain Landing, where in earlier times steamboats often had trouble mooring.

Caddo Lake at Uncertain. Courtesy of Ray Miller.

UNIVERSAL CITY
South Texas • Bexar County • 14,842

Universal City, a town providing services and housing to the Randolph Air Force Base area, incorporated in 1960. A real estate developer chose the town name, saying it emphasized the air base's universal importance.

UTOPIA
Southwest Texas • Uvalde County • 360

Captain William Ware, a soldier in the revolutionary army of Texas, moved to Sabinal Canyon in 1852 and founded the village of Waresville. His son-in-law, Robert Kincheloe, brought his family to the area in 1873, built a home, platted a new townsite near Waresville, and donated lots for a public square, a school, and churches. The Waresville post office moved to the new townsite in 1883. Postmaster George Barker had its name changed to Utopia, a name given by Sir Thomas More, the sixteenth-century poet and humanist, to an imaginary land of perfection.

UVALDE
Southwest Texas • Uvalde County • 16,155 • yoo-VAL-dee

Reading W. Black founded this town in 1853 and named it Encina. Three years later it became the county seat and was renamed Uvalde for Juan de Ugalde, the Spanish governor who led troops to victory over 300 Apaches in a 1790 battle at Sabinal Canyon. A post office opened in 1857, and the Galveston, Harrisburg & San Antonio Railway reached here in 1881. Uvalde was incorporated in 1888 with a population nearing 2,000. John Nance "Cactus Jack" Garner, who served 15 terms in Congress, and two terms as Franklin Roosevelt's vice president, first came to Uvalde in 1890. He moved back after retiring from public office in 1941. Another Uvalde resident was Dale Evans, born here in 1912.

VALENTINE
Far west Texas • Jeff Davis County • 261

Railroad construction workers, laying track for a Southern Pacific line, reached this distant point in West Texas on St. Valentine's Day, 1882. They decided that the townsite being established here should be named Valentine.

VAN

Northeast Texas • Van Zandt County • 2,194

Pioneer settlers came here around the Civil War years, but this town was officially founded during the 1890s. Henry Vance opened the first post office in 1894. It took the name Van, for postmaster Vance and resident Vannie Tunnell. Van was a quiet farming town until the Van oil field was discovered in 1929. Pure Oil and other major companies controlled most of the field's acreage, but J. A. Bracken, whose farm was in the middle of the field, refused offers to lease his land. Instead, he drilled it himself—and eventually had millions to show for it.

VANDERBILT

Gulf Coast • Jackson County • 618

Vanderbilt was established in 1904 at a station on the St. Louis, Brownsville & Mexico Railway. Its post office opened in 1907. According to local lore, the post office was named for the heroic captain of a cotton barge sunk near the mouth of the Navidad River shortly before the Civil War ended.

VENUS

Central Texas • Johnson County • 1,209

Settlers came to this area as early as the 1850s, but three decades passed before J. C. Smyth bought 80 acres of land and platted a townsite here. He named the town in honor of Venus Housley, the daughter of a local doctor. When the post office opened in 1888, it operated for several weeks under the name Gossip before its name was changed to Venus.

VERIBEST

West central Texas • Tom Green County • 40

The community of Mullins, which sprang up here in the early 1900s, was named for pioneer settler Isaac Mullins, who contributed some of his land for a school and a cemetery. But in 1926 postal officials in Washington wouldn't accept Mullins as a name for the town's post office. They thought it would be confused with the Mullin post office in Mills County. According to a local historian, Veribest, the substitute name proposed and accepted, was drawn from a packing company's brand name and logo.

VERNON
Oklahoma border • Wilbarger County • 12,496

The name of the townsite established here in 1880 was meant to be Eagle Flat. Postal officials, however, pointed out that Texas already had post offices named Eagle Lake and Eagle Pass. Instead they named the town's post office Vernon, after George Washington's Mount Vernon estate on the Potomac River.

VICTORIA
Gulf Coast • Victoria County • 61,348

Few other settlers lived in this area in 1824 when Martin De Leon established a colony here, naming it Guadalupe Victoria for the first president of the republic of Mexico. After gaining independence from Mexico, Texas incorporated the town of Victoria in 1839. The *Victoria Advocate* was founded in 1846 and still publishing in 1998.

VIDOR
Louisiana border • Orange County • 11,352 • VYE-der

This community evolved from the logging camp of the Miller-Vidor Lumber Company in 1907 and was named for company founder Charles S. Vidor. After logging operations ended in the 1920s, the community's economy shifted to cattle raising, cotton, and rice.

VON ORMY
South Texas • Bexar County • 264

When a post office opened in this small settlement in 1879, it was named Manns' Crossing, for the family who operated a ferry at the Medina River nearby. In 1886, the name was changed to honor Adolph von Ormy, an Austrian count who, the year before, bought 2,300 acres of land here. The estate had belonged to the late Enoch Jones, a wealthy San Antonio merchant and land speculator, and included the two-story stone mansion Jones built in 1854—said to be the first Texas residence equipped with a complete indoor plumbing system. The count and countess arrived accompanied by some 20 liveried servants. But the countess returned to Europe after only one year in Texas, and a year later Count von Ormy vanished under mysterious circumstances.

WACO

Central Texas • McLennan County • 109,296 • WAY-koh

The Waco Indians lived in this area before being displaced by Cherokees around 1830. In 1849 a townsite called Waco Village was established. Among the early settlers was Shapley Ross, a ranger who established a ferry on the Brazos River, built the town's first hotel, and became the first postmaster. The name Waco Village was shortened to Waco in 1856. Construction of a suspension bridge over the Brazos River in 1870 and the arrival of three railroads by the early 1880s spurred Waco's growth, as did Baylor University's move here in 1887. The town's progress was symbolized by the 22-story Amicable Insurance building, the tallest building in Texas at its completion in 1911. Actor Steve Martin is a Waco native.

WARDA

Central Texas • Fayette County • 98

Wendish immigrants established a community here in the 1860s and 1870s, bringing customs and culture from their Slavic enclave in the center of Prussia. They named the community for Wartha, Saxony, the former home of A. F. Falke, the first settler here and proprietor of the general store established in 1874. Holy Cross Lutheran Church was founded in 1882. Through the years, the church has been the center of this farming community, whose population is still principally made up of the original settlers' descendants.

WASHINGTON

Southeast Texas • Washington County • 265

In 1833 Dr. Ada Hoxey named this frontier village Washington, for the Georgia town where he lived before coming to Texas. Merchants and tradesmen were attracted by the town's location on the bluffs above the Brazos River. Late in 1835, Washington became the headquarters of General Sam Houston's Texas army, and, in an assembly hall here, Houston and others signed the Texas Declaration of Independence, wrote a constitution, and organized the government of the Republic of Texas. The town was also capital of the republic in the last years before Texas joined the United States. In the 1850s Washington, also known as Washington-on-the-Brazos, became a prosperous cotton-shipping riverport. Preferring to depend upon their profitable river trade, local leaders declined to give railroads the bonuses they sought in exchange for routing their trains through this town. As a result, trains were routed to other towns instead, and railroad competition soon killed steamboat traffic on the Brazos. Bypassed by the railroads, Washington saw its population fall from an estimated 4,000 in 1860 to about 200 by 1885.

WATAUGA

North central Texas • Tarrant County • 21,900 • wuh-TAW-guh

Watauga's name, a Cherokee word, is said to mean "village of many springs." This settlement originally consisted of scattered farm and ranch homes. Their residents became an organized community after the Texas & Pacific Railway built a station in this area in 1882, and a post office opened in 1883. Watauga remained small and rural until aircraft plants began to open in the vicinity during World War II. Fort Worth's metropolitan growth also brought thousands of new residents to the town.

WATER VALLEY

West central Texas • Tom Green County • 120

David Williams, one of the earliest ranchers to settle in the North Concho River valley, founded this town in the early 1880s and obtained permission to open a post office. It was named Yandell for a San Angelo doctor. After Williams died in 1886, the post office moved to Ben Mayes' store. Mayes tried to change the name from Yandell to Xerifaville in honor of his new bride, Xerifa, but bowed to a storm of protest from townspeople who claimed they could hardly pronounce the name, much less spell it. John Hanson, who replaced Mayes as postmaster in 1889, won approval of a new name for both the town and post office: Water Valley, the name of the Mississippi town where he was born.

WAXAHACHIE

Central Texas • Ellis County • 20,350 • wawks-uh-HATCH-ih

Waxahachie's name derives from a Tonkawa Indian word meaning "cow (or buffalo) creek." Emory W. Rogers, a pioneer settler who built a log cabin on Waxahachie Creek in 1847, donated land for the townsite. A post office and a general store opened in 1850, Waxahachie became the Ellis County seat, and a county courthouse was built. The Waxahachie Tap Railroad, completed in 1879, carried more than 5,000 bales of cotton from Waxahachie, and brought more than 140 carloads of lumber into the town, in its initial 12 months of operation.

WEATHERFORD

North central Texas • Parker County • 17,503

Weatherford was named for Jefferson Weatherford, the state senator from Dallas who sponsored a bill to create Parker County in 1855. The town was incorporated in 1858. During Weatherford's first 25 years, its citizens often provided refuge for other Parker County residents during Indian raids. Railroads arrived here in the 1880s and 1890s, and the town has grown steadily ever since.

WEBSTER
Southeast Texas • Harris County • 5,337

James W. Webster brought a group of English colonists here around 1880 to settle this site, which he called Gardentown. The town was later renamed for Webster. It became the cradle of the huge Gulf Coast rice industry in the early 1900s, thanks to Seito Saibara, who came to America from Japan for graduate studies and, in 1903, accepted an invitation from the Houston Chamber of Commerce to teach rice cultivation to Harris County farmers. He had a 1,000-acre tract planted in Shinriki seed, a superior variety of rice, and seed from the first harvest was distributed to Texas and Louisiana farmers. Webster remained a small farming community until the 1960s, when construction of the NASA space center caused a local population boom.

WEIMAR
Southeast Texas • Colorado County • 2,253 • WYE-mer

Anticipating that the Galveston, Harrisburg & San Antonio railroad would arrive at this site, D. W. Jackson founded this town in 1873. Early settlers called the community Jackson, but the post office took the name Weimar, at the suggestion of settlers from Weimar, Germany, or possibly at the suggestion of a railroad official who had visited the German town and described it favorably.

WELLINGTON
Panhandle • Collingsworth County • 2,537

Soon after British cattlemen bought the nearby Rocking Horse Ranch, the promoters of this town decided to name it in honor of the first Duke of Wellington. They said they did so because a relative of one of the ranch's new owners—John Campbell Hamilton Golden, the Earl of Aberdeen—had been at Waterloo in 1815 when the Duke led England's army to victory over Napoleon. The promoters laid out the townsite in 1890 on land that had been part of the Rocking Horse, and persuaded the ranch's cowboys to vote for Wellington, instead of Pearl City, to become the seat of newly organized Collingsworth County.

WESLACO

Far south Texas • Hidalgo County • 26,503 • WES-luh-koh

In 1917 Tyler land dealer W. E. Stewart purchased 30,000 acres of land on which he established a townsite. He coined the town's name by combining several letters from the name of his W. E. Stewart Land Company.

WEST COLUMBIA

Gulf Coast • Brazoria County • 5,214

This historic town near the Gulf Coast, founded in 1826 by Josiah H. Bell, was known as Columbia when it served briefly in 1836 as capital of the Republic of Texas. General Sam Houston was inaugurated here on October 12, 1836, as the republic's first president. Five weeks later, legislators voted to move the capital to Houston, where better accommodations for government personnel were available. Growth lagged for almost a century, until the discovery of the West Columbia oil field in 1918. The town had been called West Columbia since a neighboring community changed its name from Marion to East Columbia in 1842. Josiah Bell did not record a specific reason for picking the name Columbia in 1826, but it has been a popular place name throughout American history.

WHARTON

Southeast Texas • Wharton County • 9,995

Wharton was named for two activists in the movement for Texas independence, brothers John A. Wharton and William H. Wharton. Some of Stephen F. Austin's colonists settled the town in 1846, the same year Wharton County—also named for the two brothers—was organized. Wharton is the birthplace of journalist Dan Rather.

WHEELOCK

East central Texas • Robertson County • 125

Eleazer L. R. Wheelock established this town in 1833 and named it for Wheelock, Vermont, which was named for his grandfather, the founder of Dartmouth College. Wheelock lost its bid to be chosen as the state capital—by a single vote, according to a local historian—and was also turned down as a prospective site for the University of Texas. It became the county seat in

1850, but Owensville replaced it in 1856. When Wheelock was then bypassed by railroads in the late 1860s and 1870s, many residents moved away.

WHITEFACE
New Mexico border • Cochran County • 490

C. C. Slaughter named the Whiteface Camp and Whiteface Pasture on his ranch for the white-faced Hereford cattle grazing there, and the name in turn was given to this town. Residents of the Whiteface townsite moved four or five miles to a new location established while construction workers built the South Plains & Santa Fe Railway line here in 1925.

WHITEHOUSE
Northeast Texas • Smith County • 5,226

Settled in the middle of the nineteenth century, Whitehouse took its name from a whitewashed building near the town's railroad tracks. Passengers were always told that the steam locomotive would stop "next to the white house" to replenish its water supply.

WHON
Central Texas • Coleman County • 15

This community's name is a phonetic spelling of Juan, the name of a well-regarded McCain Ranch cowboy. Seeking a short name for the post office being established here in 1903, Mrs. Sam McCain, who was appointed postmaster, proposed Whon.

WICHITA FALLS
Oklahoma border • Wichita County • 101,800

A townsite was established here in 1876 on land John A. Scott had bought 39 years earlier. It consisted of a town square, several streets with residential lots, and a segment of the Wichita River with a small waterfall that later disappeared. Wichita Falls grew into a successful railroad and oil town.

WIERGATE
Louisiana border • Newton County • 461 • WEER-gayt

Lumberman Robert W. Wier of Houston built the last large lumber mill in East Texas at this location and established Wiergate, a company town, around the end of World War I. Besides homes for Wier's employ-

Sawmill operations at Wiergate. Courtesy of T. P. Wier, Jr.

ees, the town included a company-owned commissary, two schools, two community centers, a movie theater, an ice house, and a depot for the Gulf & Northern Railroad. The railroad, also a Wier operation, connected Wiergate with the Orange & Northwestern rail line at Newton, 15 miles away. Population exceeded 2,000 in the 1920s, but the town was effectively "downsized" when, in 1943, the big sawmill closed and the railroad was abandoned. A smaller mill provided employment in Wiergate during the second half of the century.

WIMBERLEY
South central Texas • Hays County • 2,842

This retirement and resort community was named for Pleasant Wimberley, a Civil War veteran who bought John Cude's gristmill and sawmill on Cypress Creek in 1874. Residents first called the area Wimberley's Mill. Growth was slow until the middle of the twentieth century, when

Wimberley started to become a popular place for artists, authors, and tourists.

WINDOM

Oklahoma border • Fannin County • 308

Historians offer two stories about the origin of Windom's name. According to one version, this town was named for a Texas & Pacific railroad conductor, Thomas H. Windom. The other version attributes the name to the area's windswept terrain. Windom was established around 1880, and its post office opened in 1885. Two years later, the Rayburn family, including five-year-old Sam, arrived from Tennessee and acquired a 40-acre farm where the future Speaker of the U.S. House of Representatives grew up.

ROY ORBISON DAY
STATION
Wink, Texas 79789
JUNE 5, 1993

WINK

New Mexico border • Winkler County • 1,158

Winkler County was formed in 1887 and named for Clinton McK. Winkler, a Texas Court of Appeals judge who served in the Confederate Army. This town developed after discovery of the nearby Hendrick Oil Field in 1926. When postal officials rejected the name Winkler, a post office opened in 1927 with the shortened name Wink. Singer Roy Orbison was raised in Wink.

WODEN

East Texas • Nacogdoches County • 70

A rural hamlet, settled here a decade or more before the Civil War, was known first as Jacobs and later as King's Store. According to a local historian, Anna Green suggested the name Woden in 1886 when the community's post office was being established. In mythology, Woden is an Anglo-Saxon deity, counterpart to the Scandinavian supreme god Odin, with special skills in magic and authority over agriculture, wisdom, war, and poetry.

WOODVILLE
Southeast Texas • Tyler County • 4,061

Woodville, the Tyler County seat since 1846, was named for George T. Wood, who served with distinction as a colonel in the Mexican War and became the second governor of Texas. From the mid-nineteenth century well into the twentieth century, sawmill operations were the mainstay of Woodville's economy.

WYLIE
North central Texas • Collin, Rockwall, and Dallas counties • 11,550

Settlers formed a community in this vicinity in the 1870s and called it Nickelville. Anxious to have access to a railroad, they moved a half mile north in 1886 to the newly constructed Gulf, Colorado & Santa Fe tracks and renamed their town for the railroad's right-of-way agent, W. D. Wylie.

YANCEY
Southwest Texas • Medina County • 202

Settled in the 1890s, this town received its name because the townsite's two developers each had a son name Yancey. Yancey's population peaked around the start of World War I at 350.

YOAKUM
South Texas • Lavaca and DeWitt counties • 6,467

Yoakum was founded in 1887, when the San Antonio & Aransas Pass Railway built its tracks through this area. It was named for Benjamin F. Yoakum, the railroad's general manager and a leading figure in the fledgling Texas railroad industry.

YORKTOWN
South Texas • DeWitt County • 2,359

Charles Eckhardt and Texas Ranger Captain John York established a trading post at this site around 1847. The next year, York died while fighting Indians, and a townsite developed at the trading post was named

Yorktown. The townsite soon attracted new settlers, and Eckhardt established the town's first store, Charles Eckhardt & Sons.

ZAPATA
Far south Texas • Zapata County • 8,088 • zuh-PAH-tuh

The town that developed here in the late eighteenth century was first known as Habitacion, later Carrizo, Bellville, and San Bartolo, then once again as Carrizo. It was named Zapata in 1898, after Colonel Antonio Zapata, a politically powerful rancher who opposed Mexican president Santa Anna as a despot and attempted to create an independent Republic of the Rio Grande. Zapata was captured, convicted of treason, and executed in 1840. Because of the similarity of their names, he is sometimes confused with the early-twentieth-century Mexican revolutionary Emiliano Zapata.

ZAVALLA
East Texas • Angelina County • 815 • zuh-VAL-uh

Zavalla, which lies within the boundary of Angelina National Forest, was named in honor of Lorenzo de Zavala, who signed the Texas Declaration of Independence and served as the first president of the Texas republic. When this town was established on the Texas & New Orleans Railroad in 1900, by error its name was spelled with an extra "l."

ZEPHYR
Central Texas • Brown County • 198

Trapped here by a blue norther in 1850, a team of surveyors facetiously called this place Zephyr, a word meaning "gentle breeze." In 1870 the town of Zephyr was established. It was a flourishing trade center with a population of 1,000 when a tornado hit in 1909, killing 32 residents. Although churches, schools, businesses, and homes were rebuilt, Zephyr failed to regain its peak population.

Index of Counties

Anderson County, 63, 133, 146, 187
Andrews County, 7
Angelina County, 56, 116, 204
Aransas County, 8, 73, 165
Archer County, 9, 88, 175
Atascosa County, 36, 155, 157
Austin County, 17, 22, 34, 92, 138,
    172, 175

Bailey County, 38, 131
Bandera County, 13, 154
Bastrop County, 14, 63
Bee County, 16, 140, 149, 190
Bell County, 18, 57, 101, 186
Bexar County, 37, 44, 85, 109, 169,
    170, 174, 192, 194
Blanco County, 22, 91, 95
Borden County, 74
Bosque County, 40, 124
Bowie County, 53, 136, 161, 188
Brazoria County, 5, 7, 25, 40, 72, 105,
    118, 143, 149, 167, 199
Brazos County, 28, 41, 127
Brewster County, 4, 118, 182, 187
Briscoe County, 160, 177
Brooks County, 67
Brown County, 14, 22, 28, 188, 204
Burleson County, 30
Burnet County, 30, 119

Caldwell County, 113, 117, 157
Calhoun County, 157
Cameron County, 27, 43, 83, 104, 115,
    156, 171
Camp County, 154
Cass County, 11, 58

Castro County, 57, 133
Chambers County, 6, 175
Cherokee County, 5, 49, 94, 122,
    162, 169
Childress County, 36, 186
Clay County, 17, 85, 95, 151, 175
Cochran County, 200
Coke County, 26, 164, 187
Collin County, 3, 34, 68, 73, 123, 136,
    154, 162, 203
Collingsworth County, 57, 198
Colorado County, 4, 42, 132, 141, 198
Comal County, 136, 174
Comanche County, 43, 65
Concho County, 61, 66, 145
Cooke County, 66, 74, 131
Coryell County, 45, 68, 76, 147,
    158, 190
Cottle County, 34, 145
Crane County, 47
Crockett County, 144

Dallam County, 34, 51
Dallas County, 1, 13, 33, 44, 51, 55,
    58, 76, 80, 93, 106, 125, 162, 168,
    175, 203
Dawson County, 106
Deaf Smith County, 52, 86
Delta County, 19, 44, 102
Denton County, 9, 11, 44, 54, 69, 80,
    110, 152, 164, 172
DeWitt County, 49, 203
Dickens County, 180
Dimmitt County, 33
Donley County, 38, 84, 109
Duval County, 18, 72, 161, 171

Eastland County, 32, 38, 55, 60, 160, 163
Ector County, 140, 141, 150
El Paso County, 8, 32, 64, 67, 171
Ellis County, 12, 34, 65, 93, 118, 122, 126, 146, 161, 162, 197
Erath County, 59, 181

Falls County, 119, 166
Fannin County, 24, 29, 88, 94, 104, 139,185, 202
Fayette County, 32, 69, 104, 168, 195
Floyd County, 69
Fort Bend County, 73, 82, 92, 129, 135, 144, 163, 166, 180, 182
Franklin County, 131, 184
Freestone County, 58, 67
Frio County, 19, 149

Gaines County, 114, 176
Galveston County, 12, 56, 73, 74, 86, 87, 99, 105, 108, 156, 175
Garza County, 97, 157
Gillespie County, 72, 181
Glasscock County, 76
Goliad County, 67, 78
Gonzales County, 16, 47, 79
Gray County, 2, 146
Grayson County, 17, 42, 54, 176
Gregg County, 78, 101, 114
Grimes County, 7, 92, 133
Guadalupe County, 37, 77, 174, 176

Hale County, 82, 154
Hall County, 105, 123
Hamilton County, 67, 83
Hardeman County, 36, 159
Hardin County, 103, 117, 174, 179
Harris County, 3, 14, 15, 17, 35, 48, 53, 73, 74, 87, 88, 90, 94, 98, 107, 108, 129, 148, 175, 180, 189, 198
Harrison County, 65, 97, 120, 191
Hartley County, 35, 51
Haskell County, 83
Hays County, 28, 59, 103, 172, 201
Hemphill County, 31

Henderson County, 11, 82, 117
Hidalgo County, 2, 5, 58, 61, 65, 86, 111, 115, 122, 124, 128, 150, 152, 172, 199
Hill County, 21, 87, 90, 94, 130
Hockley County, 110, 151, 166, 168, 183
Hood County, 80, 112
Hopkins County, 152, 182
Houston County, 48, 100
Howard County, 21, 41, 70
Hudspeth County, 53, 177
Hunt County, 43, 81, 125
Hutchinson County, 24

Jack County, 94
Jackson County, 61, 72, 75, 108, 113, 193
Jasper County, 29, 66, 95, 102
Jeff Davis County, 70, 192
Jefferson County, 5, 30, 40, 96, 98, 111, 118, 193
Jim Hogg County, 84
Jim Wells County, 3, 18
Johnson County, 5, 30, 40, 96, 98, 111, 118, 192
Jones County, 8, 12

Karnes County, 60, 98, 99, 147
Kaufman County, 70, 98, 187
Kendall County, 23, 43, 99, 178
Kenedy County, 10
Kent County, 155
Kerr County, 100, 130
Kimble County, 96, 114, 166, 185
Kleberg County, 101, 164
Knox County, 102

La Salle County, 47, 65
Lamar County, 23, 148, 151
Lamb County, 6, 60, 112, 182
Lampasas County, 106, 113
Lavaca County, 82, 177, 183, 203
Lee County, 56, 77, 110
Leon County, 28, 109, 140
Liberty County, 40, 50, 52, 110
Limestone County, 19, 81, 125
Live Oak County, 57, 77

Llano County, 112
Loving County, 124
Lubbock County, 91, 116, 137, 178
Lynn County, 138

Madison County, 117, 140
Marion County, 95, 113
Martin County, 113, 181, 184
Mason County, 10, 120
Matagorda County, 15, 22, 41, 63,
    120, 146
Maverick County, 59, 160
McCulloch County, 25
McLennan County, 17, 64, 86, 123,
    167, 195
McMullen County, 188
Medina County, 33, 55, 56, 88, 132, 203
Menard County, 123
Midland County, 126
Milam County, 18, 31, 52, 165, 188
Mitchell County, 42
Montague County, 24, 139, 169, 183
Montgomery County, 44, 50, 137, 180
Moore County, 30, 59
Morris County, 50, 114, 143
Motley County, 69, 120

Nacogdoches County, 37, 58, 66, 132,
    169, 202
Navarro County, 23, 45
Newton County, 24, 56, 138, 200
Nolan County, 139, 183
Nueces County, 2, 14, 21, 45, 156, 164

Ochiltree County, 151
Orange County, 25, 144, 194

Palo Pinto County, 79, 127, 146, 174
Panola County, 33, 76, 147
Parker County, 127, 189, 197
Parmer County, 24, 67, 73, 108
Pecos County, 70, 91, 93
Polk County, 1, 45, 112, 130, 143
Potter County, 6
Presidio County, 119, 158

Rains County, 2
Randall County, 32, 83
Reagan County, 21, 188
Real County, 31, 109
Red River County, 7, 23, 39
Reeves County, 13, 150
Refugio County, 162
Roberts County, 126
Robertson County, 84, 199
Rockwall County, 67, 165, 168, 203
Runnels County, 13
Rusk County, 85, 105, 131, 162

Sabine County, 126
San Augustine County, 170
San Jacinto County, 155
San Patricio County, 8, 92, 121, 141,
    156, 184
San Saba County, 36
Schleicher County, 63
Scurry County, 178
Shackelford County, 3
Shelby County, 35
Sherman County, 181
Smith County, 10, 190, 200
Somervell County, 78, 135, 160
Starr County, 54, 75, 104, 163, 165, 173
Stephens County, 25, 82, 133
Stonewall County, 142
Sutton County, 178
Swisher County, 83, 190

Tarrant County, 9, 12, 16, 19, 41, 49,
    66, 71, 80, 91, 99, 100, 118, 136
Taylor County, 1, 29, 144, 190
Terry County, 26, 189
Titus County, 131
Tom Green County, 32, 37, 102, 164,
    193, 197
Travis County, 11, 117, 151
Tyler County, 36, 42, 87, 203

Upshur County, 78
Upton County, 122
Uvalde County, 43, 192

Val Verde County, 54, 106
Van Zandt County, 19, 31, 80, 193
Victoria County, 92, 141, 160, 185, 194

Walker County, 90, 138
Waller County, 26, 85, 98, 149, 158
Ward County, 130, 158, 168
Washington County, 25, 196
Webb County, 28, 107, 142
Wharton County, 52, 60, 61, 62, 112,
   152, 199
Wheeler County, 129, 176
Wichita County, 30, 63, 93, 97, 200
Wilbarger County, 142, 194

Willacy County, 161
Williamson County, 77, 109, 111, 167,
   185, 334
Wilson County, 69, 103, 147
Winkler County, 100, 202
Wise County, 26, 53, 136, 148
Wood County, 2, 84, 127

Yoakum County, 55
Young County, 80, 116, 137, 143

Zapata County, 114, 204
Zavala County, 49

Index of Names

Abercrombie, James S., 143
Abernathy, Monroe, 137
Ackerman, Mrs. B. F., 165
Adams, Charles G., 178
Adams, H. A., 112
Allen, Ebenezer, 3
Allen, John K. and Augustus, 88
Allen, Reese, 97
Alvarez de Pineda, Alonso, 45
Ameen, E. S., 55
Anahwa, Chief, 6
Anderson, Bill, 148
Anderson, Kenneth L., 7
Anderson, Tom, 163
Andrews, Richard, 7
Angle, Mrs. George, 7
Archer, Dr. Branch T., 8
Ariola, Edward, 92
Armstrong, John B., 10
Arnold, B. T. and Bennie, 18
Arp, Bill, 10
Arthur, Chester, 36
Austin, John, 25
Austin, Stephen F., 11, 25, 28, 56, 120,
    155, 171
Avriett, Dulcena, 11
Aylor, T. W., 144

Bair, W. G., 16
Balch, John, and family, 13
Balch, William, 5
Balcom, E. D., 13
Baldwin, W. W., 17
Ball, Thomas Henry, 189
Ballinger, William Pitt, 13
Bangs, Samuel, 14
Barker, George, 192
Barker, Josefa Augustina Flores de
    Abrego, 69
Barnes, George, 111

Barrett, Daisy, 50
Barrett, Harrison, 14
Bass, Sam, 10
Bassett, Ida and Louise, 91
Bassett, Julian M., 91
Baxter, Charlie and Will, 65
Bean, Judge Roy, 106
Bearden, J. D. T., 174
Beaumont, Jefferson, 16
Bedford, Hilory G., 57
Bee, Bernard Elliott, Sr., 16
Beeson, Benjamin, 42
Bell, Bert, 57
Bell, Josiah H., 199
Bell, Peter, 18
Bell, Thomas B. and James, 17
Bell, Z. O., 57
Benavides, Placido, 18
Benbrook, James, 19
Bennett, J. M., Jr., 108
Benson, W. S. and C. W., 5
Bernard, George, 78
Berrara, Rosendo, 84
Berry, T. J., 6
Berryman, Henry, 5
Biggs, E. E., 145
Bishop, Absalom, 53
Bishop, F. Z., 21
Black, Reading W., 192
Bledsoe, Abram, 106
Bleibler, Robert, 22
Bobo, Weldon, 16
Boegel, Philip, 14
Boerne, Ludwig, 23
Boesen, P. F., 182
Boggess, Irb, 169
Bonham, James Butler, 24
Bonner, B. F., 24
Booth, William R. and Elizabeth, 118
Borden, Gail, Jr., 74

Borger, A. P. "Ace," 24
Boston, W. J., 136
Bowen, John, 155
Bowie, James, 24
Bowles, W. B., 165
Boydstun, Benjamin, 165
Bracken, J. A., 193
Bradfield, William, 125
Brady, Peter Rainsford, 25
Braidfoot, Tom, 177
Breckinridge, John Cabell, 25
Bremond, Paul, 116
Brenham, Dr. Richard Fox, 25
Brice, Reverend J. W., 123
Britton, A. M., 120
Brontë, Charlotte, 26
Brookshire, Nathan, 26
Brown, Bill, 9
Brown, C. J., 140
Brown, Captain Henry S., 28
Brown, Joseph, 56
Brown, Joshua D., 100
Brown, Judge G. A. "Gyp," 109
Brown, Lafayette, 68
Brown, Leander "Catfish," 109
Brown, Major Jacob, 27
Brown, Otis, 93
Bryan, John Neely, 51
Bryan, Lewis, 7
Bryan, William Joel, 28
Buckingham, E. J., 49
Burleson, Rufus C., 30
Burnet, David G., 30, 49, 141
Burnett, Carol, 170
Burnett, Samuel Burk, 30
Burns, T. A., 112
Burroughs, Edgar Rice, 184

Cabeza de Vaca, Alvar, 158
Caldwell, Mathew, 30, 176
Cameron, Ewen, 30
Campbell, H. H. "Hank," 120
Campbell, Moses, 109
Campbell, Thomas M. and Maydelle, 122
Campbell, W. S., 180

Carhart, Lewis H. and Clara, 38
Carlisle, William, 143
Carmean, John, 32
Carroll, Daniel Joseph, 33
Carroll, Joe E., Sr., 28
Cartledge, R. E., 164
Cartwright, Bickham and Jerome, 21
Cartwright, R. L., 21
Castro, Henri, 33, 56
Chandler, Inch, 94
Chapin, Dennis, 61
Chatfield, Lieutenant W. H., 165
Chenoweth, Dr. C. H., 144
Chenoweth, Frank, 144
Childress, George Campbell, 36
Chireno, Jose Antonio, 37
Chittum, J. M. and Tuleta, 190
Choate, Moses, 112
Cisco, John, 38
Clark, James, 39
Clay, Henry, 85
Cleburne, Patrick R., 40
Clegg, T. J., 32
Cleveland, Charles Lander, 40
Cleveland, Grover, 101
Closner, John, 172
Cluck, Emmett, 34
Clute, John, 40
Clyde, Robert, 40
Coleman, Robert M., 41
Colley, Dr. Howard, 41
Collins, Carr P., 128
Collins, George W., 167
Collins, John, 117
Collins, L. R., 18
Collins, Mrs. L. M., 42
Colmesneil, W. T., 42
Colton, Walter, 181
Combes, Dr. Joe, 43
Connellee, Charles, 60
Conner, Lincoln Guy, 32
Conroe, Isaac, 44
Converse, James, 44
Conway, John J., 128
Cooper, L. W., 44
Coppell, George A., 44

Corley, Buna, 28
Corrigan, Pat and Douglas, 45
Cotton, J. F., 174
Cotulla, Joe, 47
Couch, Edward C., 61
Cox, Charles, 180
Crane, William Carey, 47
Crawford, Joan, 170
Crockett, David, 48, 53, 88
Cromwell, Carl, 21
Crosby, G. I., 48
Crosthwaite, J. L., 12
Crowley, S. H., 49
Cruger, William R., 3
Cude, John, 201
Cuney, Norris W., 49
Cunningham, E. H., 182
Cunningham, J. W., 111
Currie, Hugh, 83

D'Hanis, William, 56
Daingerfield, London, 50
Dale, Eva, 66
Daugherty, J. S., 60
Davila, Miguel, 52
Davis, Blooming, 23
Davis, Edgar B., 117
Davis, Henry Clay, 163
Day, I. C., 53
de la Garza, Felipe, 172
De Leon, Martin, 109, 194
de Soto, Hernando, 55
Decatur, Commodore Stephen, 53
Dechart, Eli, 10
Denison, George, 54
Denton, John B., 54
DePriest, L. G., 137
Devine, Thomas Jefferson, 55
Dewey, Admiral George, 56
DeWitt, Bart J., 169
DeWitt, Green, 79
Diboll, J. C., 56
Dickinson, John, 56
Dimmitt, W. C., 57
Dishman, James H., 43
Dissiway, Florence, 155

Dobie, J. Frank, 94
Dodson, Elmore, 57
Donaldson, Sam, 64
Doty, Christopher Columbus, 37
Doughty, Walter M. and Linn, 111
Douglass, Kelsey Harris, 58
Dremien, Martin, 158
Driscoll, Robert, Jr., 164
Duff, James C., 137
Duggan, Arthur, 112
Dumas, Louis, 59
Dupree, Joe, 94
Durrett, Rice, 83
Duvall, Martin, 8
Duwai, Chief, 58

Easterwood, Jeremiah, 98
Eastland, Captain William Mosby, 60
Eckhardt, Charles, 203
Ede, Fred, 61
Eggink, Ben, 55
Einstein, Albert, 137
Eisenhower, Dwight D., 54
Eldredge, W. T., 182
Elgin, Elijah, 165
Elgin, Robert Morris, 63
Ellis, Hugh, 143
Ellwood, Isaac, 166
Emanuel, Asa "Ace," 1
Emerson, Frank, 73
English, Levi, 33
Ennis, Colonel Cornelius, 65
Erath, George B., 30, 124
Ernst, Friedrich, 92
Escandon, Jose de, 107
Estes, Olive, 130
Euless, Adam, 66
Evans, Dale, 192
Evans, Major Ira and Ola, 127
Everman, John W., 66

Fabens, George, 67
Falke, A. F., 195
Fall, Dr. John Newton, 37
Faltin, August, 43
Fannin, Colonel James W., 68, 78

Fanthorp, Henry, 7
Farris, Newt, 50
Farwell, John V. and Charles B., 68
Feild, Julian, 118
Fitzsimmons, Bob, 106
Flato, F. W., 69
Fletcher, Donna Hooks, 58
Fletcher, Will and Joe, 140
Flores de Abrego, Don Francisco, 69
Flores, Julian, 171
Floyd, Dolphin Ward, 69
Flusche, August and Emil, 131
Forman, William, 154
Forney, Colonel John W., 70
Fort, Captain Battle and Fairy, 67
Freer, Charles and Minnie, 72
Freer, Daniel J., 72
Frnka, Frank, 132
Fulton, George Ware, 73
Fulton, Robert, 73
Furneaux, Wilson, 182

Gaines, Edmund P., 74
Galvez, Bernardo de, 74
Gandy, W. H., 50
Garcia, Luciano, 172
Garcia, Ygnacio, 75
Gardner, William, 76
Garland, A. H., 76
Garner, John Nance, 192
Garrison, Smith, 76
Gatlin, Larry, 176
George, William and Elsa, 65
Geronimo, Chief, 77
Gibbs, Barnett, 44
Giddings, DeWitt Clinton, 77
Giddings, Jabez Demming, 77
Gilmer, Thomas W., 78
Gipson, Fred, 120
Glasscock, George Washington, Sr., 77
Glidden, Joe, 6
Golden, John C. H., 198
Gonzales, Rafael, 79
Goodnight, Charles, 116
Gossett, Andrew Edward, 48
Gossett, Elijah, 48

Gould, Jay, 177
Graham, Gus and Edwin, 80
Granbury, General Hiram
        Bronson, 80
Grant, Richard, 76
Gray, Ephraim, and family, 90
Greeley, Horace, 99
Green, Anna, 202
Green, David Griggs, 130
Green, Joseph, 184
Green, Luther "Laz," 108
Green, Thomas, 81
Grinnell, Lawrence and Morgan, 102
Groesbeeck, Abram, 81
Groos, Carl, 49
Groves, John, 143
Guerra, Arcadio, 111
Guyard, Rene, 128

Hale, John C., 82
Hallett, Mrs. John, 82
Halsell, William E., 6, 60
Hamilton, James, 83
Hammond, A. L., 32
Hanson, John, 197
Hardin, John Wesley, 10
Hardy, Samuel, 137
Hargrove, A. H. and Era, 66
Harrell, Jacob, 167
Harris, L. B., 164
Harrison, Dan, 143
Hartson, Mary Kyle, 103
Harwood, Orphelia Crosby, 119
Haskell, Charles R., 83
Hawkins, William Allen, 126
Hayes, Rutherford B., 189
Hayter, Andrew, 10
Hearne, Christopher Columbus, 84
Hebbron, James R., 84
Hedley, J. E. M., 85
Hellman, Ben, 131
Hempstead, Dr. G. B. S., 85
Henderson, J. Pinckney, 85
Hewitt, George A., 86
Hicks, Benjamin, 171
Hidalgo y Costilla, Miguel, 86

Hill, Dr. George W., 87
Hill, Lon, Sr., and Lon, Jr., 83, 115, 122
Hilton, Conrad, 38
Hindman, Pete, 185
Hitchcock, Lent M., 87
Hoff, Fred, and family, 149
Holford, James and John, 110
Holland, Spearman, 33
Holliday, Captain John J., 88
Hollister, W. H., 86
Holly, Buddy, 116
Holt, James W., 128
Hooks, T. J., 58
Hoover, C. C. "Cohn," 57
Horner, James E., 23
Housley, Venus, 193
Houston, General Sam, 11, 53, 88, 89,
    111, 157, 168, 176, 196, 199
Howard, Robert E., 48
Howell, Joseph, 169
Hoxey, Dr. Ada, 196
Hubbard, Richard B., Jr., 90
Hull, Thomas, 76
Hungerford, Daniel E., 92
Hungerford, Inez, 92
Hunt, Joel Jefferson, 102
Hunt, R. W., and family, 102
Hurst, W. L. "Billy," 91

Ingenhuett, Peter Joseph, 43
Ingersoll, Robert Green, 161
Irving, Washington, 93, 102

Jack, Patrick C. and William H., 94
Jackson, Abner, 105
Jackson, D. W., 198
Jackson, Dr. William, 94
Jackson, Stephen, 179
Jackson, Thomas "Stonewall," 181
James, John, 23
Jarrott, Jim, 166
Jasper, Sergeant William, 95
Jefferson, Thomas, 95
Jennings, Waylon, 112
Jernigan, William, 43
Johnson, Adam, 119

Johnson, James Polk, 95
Johnson, Jimmie, 135
Johnson, Lady Bird, 98
Johnson, Lyndon B., 95, 98, 181
Joiner, C. M. "Dad," 105
Jolly, William H., 95
Jones, Curly, 4
Jones, Dr. Anson, 8
Jones, Ed, 36
Joplin, Janis, 156
Jordan, D. J., 139
Jordan, John, 80
Jordan, Thomas C., 78
Justice, Appleton, 97
Justice, Jefferson Davis, 97

Kalb, Major General Johann, 53
Karnes, Henry W., 98
Kaufman, David S., 98
Keith, Stephen, 131
Keller, John C., 99
Kelly, Bryan, 112
Kelly, John C., 152
Kelly, Myra, 1
Kemp, Joe, 97
Kempner, Isaac H., 182
Kendall, George W., 99
Kenedy, Mifflin, 99
Kennard, John E., 100
Kennedy, Oliver, 100
Kerr, James, 101
Kerr, Major James, 79
Kiber, F., 7
Kilgore, Constantine B., 101
Killeen, Frank, 101
Kimbrough, R. S., 125
Kimmison, O. M., 47
Kincheloe, Robert, 192
King, Captain Richard, 102
King, Henrietta, 164
King, M. S., 180
Kirby, John H., 66, 102
Kittrell, Norman Goree, 140
Kleberg, Robert J., 3, 34
Knight, George, 150
Knox, Henry, 102

Koch, Theodore F., 164
Kolp, D. C., 93
Konz, John Jacob, 181
Kosciusko, Major General Tadeusz, 103
Kountze, Herman and Augustus, 103
Kyle, Captain Ferguson, 103
Kyle, W. H. "Uncle Billy," 141

Lafitte, Jean, 74
Laird, S. S., 105
Lamar, Mirabeau B., 83, 148
Langtry, Lillie, 106
Lea, Margaret, 158
League, John C., 108
Leakey, John L., 109
Ledwig, Reverend Francis, 151
Lee, General Robert E., 164, 181
Leveridge, Melissa, 112
Lewis, B. W., 110
Lewis, Len, 114
Lindsey, Tant, 184
Littlefield, Major George W., 112
Lockhart, Byrd, 113
Lopresto, J., 113
Lott, Uriah, 83, 122
Loving, Oliver, 116
Lowe, Edwin Lowden, 154
Lubbock, Thomas S. and Francis R., 116
Lufkin, Abraham, 116
Lufkin, Edwin P., 116
Luling, Charles B., 117
Lynch, Judge J. A., 127

Mabray, J. N., 124
Madero, J. Francisco, 110
Madison, James, 117
Magee, Alief, 3
Maguire, Jack, 173
Mahar, Peter, 106
Mann, Ralph S., 118
Manvel, Allen, 118
Marcy, Randolph, 21
Mares, Katy, 98
Marlin, John, 119
Marshall, John, 120
Martin, Jim, 67

Martin, Steve, 195
Mathis, Thomas Henry, 121
Maxwell, Z. T., 154
Mayes, Ben and Xerifa, 197
McAllen, James Balli, 122
McAllen, John, 122
McCain, Mrs. Sam, 200
McCamey, George B., 122
McClesky, John, 160
McConnell, D. D., 163
McConnell, Thomas, 157
McCowan, Frank, 104
McDade, James W., 85
McFarland, Thomas, 171
McGregor, Dr. G. C., 123
McKinney, Collin, 123
McMillan, Dr. D. B., 96
McMurtry, Larry, 8
Menard, Michel, 75
Menchaca, Jose Antonio, 118
Merchant, C. W., 1
Meurer, John H., 175
Mexia, Enrique, and family, 125
Milam, Ben, 126
Millard, Henry, 16
Millican, Robert and Elliott, 127
Millsap, LaDonna, 104
Millsap, Tom and Dorcas, 128
Moczygemba, Father Leopold, 147
Monahan, T. J. "Pat," 130
Moody, Dan, 24
Moon, William W., 172
Moore, C. C., 187
Moore, David, 103
More, Sir Thomas, 192
Morena, Rafael, 171
Morgan, Alvin, 5
Morris, Thompson, 143
Morrow, H. R., 13
Moss, Joe, 144
Mulkey, John, 34
Mullins, Isaac, 193
Mullins, Mrs. J. L., 166
Mumme, Henry, 157
Munger, W., 97
Munson, William B., Sr., 54

Murcheson, Dr. O., 125
Murphy, Audie, 81

Nance, Charles, 59
Nash, John G., 187
Nash, Tom, 76
Navarro, Jose Antonio, 45
Nelson, Louis, 130
Newsom, Will, 34
Newton, Sergeant John, 137
Nicholson, Reginald, 132
Nickel, George, 176
Nimitz, Admiral Chester, 72
Nocona, Peta, 139
Nolan, Philip, 139
Norton, Aaron, 181
Nunez, Israel P., 181

O'Connor, Sandra Day, 64
Oatts, Thomas C., 167
Ochiltree, William B., 85
Odem, Sheriff David, 141
Ogletree, Marsden, 45
Olney, Richard, 143
Onderdonk, Gilbert, 141
Onstott, A. H., 5
Orbison, Roy, 202
Ormy, Count Adolph von, 194
Orobio y Basterra, Joaquin, 8
Orr, C. P., 10

Paduke, Chief, 145
Palmer, Dr. D. S., 146
Pancake, John R., 147
Parish, Henry and Etta, 86
Parker, Chief Quanah, 159
Parker, Cynthia Ann, 139
Parker, Daniel, 146
Parrish, J. H., 52
Patten, Minnie, 127
Pattison, James, 149
Payl, George, 164
Payne, Lelia, 109
Pearsall, Thomas W., 149
Pearson, Dr. Fred Stark, 132
Pearson, Natalie, 132

Peebles, Dr. Richard, 85
Pena, Niceforo G., Sr., 54
Penn, David, 143
Penn, Gabriel, 93
Penn, J. H., 150
Perez, Pablo, 171
Perry, George M., 151
Peters, William S., 33
Petty, J. M., 151
Peyton, Lafayette, 68
Pfluger, Henry, 151
Pharr, Henry, 152
Pierce, Abel Head "Shanghai,"
    146, 152, 153
Pierce, Jonathan E., 22
Pitts, William Harrison, 154
Pleasants, John, 155
Plehwe, Otto, 10
Post, C. W., 110, 157
Poteet, Francis Marion, 157
Poteet, H. R., 148
Powell, E. M., 144
Presswood, Austin and Sarah, 137
Price, H. L. and Cuney, 49

Ramirez, Benito, 114
Rath, Charles, 129
Rather, Dan, 199
Ratliff, John W., 57
Rauschenberg, Robert, 156
Rayburn, Sam, 202
Raymond, Edward B., 161
Reading, A. H., 144
Ready, F. M., 172
Reese, C. K. and Lolita, 113
Reeves, J. K., 160
Reeves, Jim, 33
Reisdorff, Father Joseph, 133
Renfro, G. W., 111
Renfro, Reverend H. C., 30
Reynolds, Debbie, 64
Reynolds, J. B., 102
Rhea, J. E., 13
Rhodes, Dora Collings, 139
Rice, William Marsh, 162
Richardson, A. S., 162

Richardson, E. H., 162
Rinker, A. R., 135
Ripley, Robert, 82, 189
Ritter, Tex, 33
Rivers, Channing, 35
Robertson, Sterling C., 119
Robinson, Addison, 1
Robinson, Henry, and family, 155
Robinson, Robert Ted, and family, 155
Rogers, Emory W., 197
Roman, Major Richard, 165
Roosevelt, Franklin, 137, 143
Roosevelt, Kermit, 100
Roosevelt, Theodore, 30, 166
Rosenberg, Henry, 167
Ross, L. Sullivan "Sul," 167
Ross, Shapley, 195
Rowland, Unaguy, 82
Rowlett, Daniel, 168
Rusk, Thomas Jefferson, 169

Saibara, Seito, 198
Sanborn, Henry, 6
Sanchez, Captain Tomas, 107
Sanford, Gary, 76
Santo, John Adam, 174
Sayner, Sam C., 187
Schendel, August, 135
Schertz, Sebastian, and family, 175
Schoellmann, J. W., and family, 132
Schreiner, Captain Charles, 101
Schulze, J. O., 93
Scott, Henry J., 175
Scott, John A., 200
Scott, Sir Walter, 94, 138
Seago, T. K., 175
Sealy, George, 175
Seguin, Juan Nepomuceno, 176
Shaw, James, 110
Shepherd, Albion, 118
Sherley, Andrew "Buddie," 108
Sherman, Sidney, 176
Shiner, Henry B., 177
Shoemaker, Bill, 67
Silliman, W. B., 63
Simmons, Benjamin, 19

Simmons, Charles F., 36
Singletary, S. H. and Polar, 155
Sitton, Mrs. R. L., 1
Slaton, O. L., 178
Slaughter, C. C., 200
Slaughter, R. L. "Bob," 183
Smith, Captain Edward, 65
Smith, Jackson, 94
Smith, Levi, 188
Smith, Sam, 183
Smith, Taylor, 111
Smyth, J. C., 193
Snyder, William Henry "Pete," 178
Soergel, Alwin H., 168
Solms-Braunfels, Prince Carl of, 136
Spencer, W. O., 111
St. Ambrose, Mrs. A., 105
Stafford, William, 180
Stanton, Edward McMasters, 181
Stati, John Santo, 174
Stephen, John M. and William, 181
Sterling, Ross, 90
Stevens, R. S., 54
Stevenson, Robert and Coke R., 114
Stewart, Clayton, 70
Stewart, Dr. Azle, 12
Stewart, Dr. Thomas H. DeSoto, 55
Stewart, George, 164
Stewart, W. E., 199
Stillwell, Arthur E., 155
Stinebaugh, Granville, 136
Strake, George, 44
Study, Will, 182
Sydnor, John and Seabrook, 175

Taft, Charles, 184
Taft, William Howard, 184
Taylor, Allen, 166
Taylor, Aubrey and Eura, 130
Taylor, Edward M., 185
Taylor, General Zachary, 27, 53,
Telfener, Count Joseph, 61, 92, 185
Temple, Bernard M., 186
Temple, Thomas L. L., 56
Tennyson, Alfred, 187
Teran de los Rios, Domingo, 170

Terrell, Robert A., 187
Thiessen, Gus, 23
Thigpen, Dr. Benjamin J., 32
Tilden, Samuel J., 189
Todd, Madison L., 150
Trammel, May Pearl, 122
Trent, I. R., 190
Trevino, Jesus, 174
Truss, John, 28
Tucker, Tanya, 176
Tuffing, Arthur, and family, 97
Tunnell, Vannie, 193
Turner, Amasa, 141
Tweedy, Joseph, 102
Twitchell, W. D., 3
Twohig, John, 60
Tyler, John, 190
Tyng, George, 146

Ugalde, Juan de, 192
Unzicker, Peter, 190
Upshur, Abel, 78

Van Zandt, Isaac, 120
Vance, Henry, 193
Victoria, Guadalupe, 94
Vidor, Charles S., 194
Viesca, Augustin, 119
Vineyard, J. W., 92
Vinson, Charles, 131
Von Froelich, Gerri, 125
Von Roeder, Ludwig and Leopold, 34

Waggoner, W. B., 166
Waggoner, William T. and Electra, 63
Walker, George W., 7
Walker, Margaret L., 162
Wallace, William "Bigfoot," 19, 20
Ward, Lafayette, 108
Ware, Captain William, 192

Ware, Mrs. H. D., 189
Warren, Charles and Ed, 132
Washington, George, 194
Watts, P. S., 174
Weatherford, Jefferson, 197
Webster, James W., 198
Wellington, Duke of, 198
West, George Washington, 77
Wharton, John A. and William H., 199
Wheeler, Benjamin F., 19
Wheelock, Eleazer L. R., 199
Whetstone, Peter, 120
Whitbread, Walter, 112
White, Etta, 50
Wier, Robert W., 24, 200
Williams, David, 197
Wilson, S. J., 182
Wimberley, Pleasant, 201
Windham, Trav, 150
Windom, Thomas H., 202
Winkler, Clinton McK., 202
Wood, George T., 203
Wood, H. W., 99
Wooten, Dr. George G., 7
Works, Joe "Buckskin," 142
Worth, General William Jenkins, 71
Wright, Bob, 129
Wright, George W., 148
Wright, George, 73
Wylie, W. D., 203

Yates, Ira and Ann, 93
Yoakum, Benjamin F., 203
York, Captain John, 203
Young, John, 61, 86, 122

Zaharias, Babe, 156
Zapata, Colonel Antonio, 204
Zavala, Lorenzo de, 204
Zink, Nicolaus, 136, 178

About the Authors

Bill Bradfield published *Financial Trend*, a Southwestern business newsweekly, for a dozen years, and earlier was editor of Dallas-area daily and weekly suburban newspapers. He is a member of the Texas State Historical Association and Sigma Delta Chi, Society of Professional Journalists. **Clare Bradfield** is a former reporter for the *Garland News*. Both are life-long residents of Texas towns.